SEVEN ESSENTIALS
— *for the* —
SPIRITUAL JOURNEY

SEVEN
ESSENTIALS
— for the —
SPIRITUAL
JOURNEY

DOLORES R. LECKEY

A *Crossroad* Book
The Crossroad Publishing Company
New York

The Crossroad Publishing Company
370 Lexington Avenue, New York, NY 10017

Printed in the United States of America

Library of Congress Cataloging-in-Publication Data

Leckey, Dolores R.
    Seven essentials for the spiritual journey / by Dolores R. Leckey.
       p.   cm.
    Includes bibliographical references.
    ISBN 0-8245-1783-0 (pbk.)
    1. Spiritual life – Catholic Church.   I. Title.
  BX2350.2.L43 1999
  248.4'82 – dc21   98-46774

1 2 3 4 5 6 7 8 9 10   04 03 02 01 00 99

To the many communities of women and men
who are my companions on the journey:

- *The Benedictine monks of St. Anselm Abbey, Washington, D.C.*

- *The discalced Carmelite nuns who quietly and creatively inspire, drawing souls to the spirit of God.*

- *The Dominican friars of the Southern Province, U.S.A.*

- *The Jesuit community at the Woodstock Theological Center, Washington, D.C.*

- *The Shalem Institute for Spiritual Formation, Bethesda, Md.*

- *The Trappist monks of Holy Cross Abbey, Berryville, Va.*

With a grateful heart

CONTENTS

Foreword

I have known Dolores Leckey as a friend and colleague for
more than twenty-five years. She was one of the pioneering
souls who participated in the first long-term spiritual exploration
group in 1973 of what later became the Shalem Institute for Spiritual Formation. In the years since then I have been in touch
with many facets of her inspiring journey of human and spiritual
exploration, fidelity, and action. I have marveled at the incredible
range of people, places, and events that she has encountered over
these years, many of which have helped to define the high-water
marks of the church's and society's life of these last decades. She
has retained an openness and responsiveness through her public and private life that have kept her in the hands of the living
Spirit. She has been willing to learn not only from the deep traditional sources of the church's riches, but also from those of
other traditions and many contemporary writers, as well as her
own rich inner spiritual life. It is from the wells of this deep
and broad experience that the basic spiritual wisdom of this fine
book flows.

Someone who has been willing to live on so many frontiers
of spiritual thought and action in our time is an inspiration for
our own willingness to live on the leading edge of the Spirit's
movements among us. As all of us know who have tried to
live in the bare light of this edge, it can be very demanding,
disorienting, and lonely, as well as consoling. Sorting out what
really is essential in the life of the Spirit and what turns out
to be chaff can be a very difficult and lengthy process. This is
especially true in a societal time of such ongoing fundamental

change and challenge, both within and outside of the religious community.

For both spiritual beginners and those more mature along the spiritual path, it is very helpful to find an experienced, wise teacher who can remind us of the fundamentals of a sane spiritual life amid the volatility of our contemporary world. The seven essentials for spiritual growth that Dolores Leckey offers us provide just such a sifting out of the really vital dimensions of a spiritual life that seeks the truth of God, self, and community. She presents these dimensions with the help not only of her own seasoned personal experience but also that of many of the greatest spiritual leaders of our time, some of them well known and some of them blessed ordinary people.

Dolores Leckey implicitly recognizes that none of us can live in a fully enclosed religious ghetto today. The living Spirit is calling us to an appreciation of spiritual truth wherever it shows itself in our global village and to letting that truth broaden and deepen our own faith tradition. The full catholicity of the church I think requires such an appreciation. Dolores Leckey is willing to widen the inspirational resources for traditional Christian faith by including selected spiritual insights of those outside the faith, while at the same time remaining confidently grounded in the graced heart of Christian tradition.

In doing so she reflects the powerful insight of Simone Weil when she said that Christ is the truth, and therefore wherever the truth is found, Christ can't be far away. Dolores Leckey speaks to the kind of probing modern church person who wants to be faithful to the living Spirit's presence both in and outside of the institutional church.

Dolores Leckey offers us the foundational practical attitudes and disciplines that we all need to incorporate in our lives if we are to realize and live out fully who we are, which the Jesuit Teilhard de Chardin well defined as "spiritual beings on a human journey, not human beings on a spiritual journey." She honors this core of our spiritual being throughout her book. If we all shared such a respect for our spiritual heart and let our way be lit by the essentials she so lucidly advocates, the church and the world would be truer to our deepest calling and community in God.

TILDEN EDWARDS

Director, Shalem Institute
for Spiritual Formation

Acknowledgments

I AM GRATEFUL to Michael Leach, who was my editor at the Crossroad Publishing Company, for suggesting that I turn a baccalaureate address, which I delivered at Lafayette College, into a small book. The writing provided a wonderful bridge from my intensely active life at the National Conference of Catholic Bishops to the quieter, more reflective life of a senior fellow at the Woodstock Theological Center. I appreciate, too, Michael's clear and helpful advice as the project developed.

The College of Preachers, on the grounds of Washington's National Cathedral, graciously welcomed me as a scholar-in-residence during the winter of 1998. Dr. Erica Ward and her staff provided quiet space and support as the book came into being. The spirit of the cathedral close was not only encouraging but inspiring.

A number of people read the first draft and invested time, energy, and expertise in their responses. To James L. Connor, S.J., Dr. John Borelli, Ruth Druhan, Margaret Kabalin Leckey, and Rhoda Nary my sincere thanks for your careful, thoughtful critique.

Finally, Bonnie Teresa Stallings brought her technical skills to the final manuscript. As always, she has been generous in many, many ways.

Introduction

Ask and it will be given to you;
seek and you will find;
knock and the door will be opened to you.

(Matthew 7:7)

For a very long time I have been conscious of being on a journey of sorts, a pilgrimage that is leading me to a destination that I dimly perceive to be "home." In the complex and exquisite web of existence — relationships, home, work, church, world — there have been lamps of wisdom, the experience of others, personal instincts, the generosity of fellow pilgrims to light the way to this final destination.

For twenty years I served as an executive with the National Conference of Catholic Bishops, a position which brought me into contact with some of the outstanding leaders of the church (understood in the widest sense) throughout the world. It also introduced me to the journeys of ordinary believers, people with extraordinary spiritual sensibilities. Their stories mingle with my own in this account of what I present as essential for an enlightened spiritual journey.

Most readers, I feel sure, can easily name the absolute essentials for human life on earth: water, air, food. Others might include shelter and safety. Still others would mention language, affection, education, meaningful work, leisure. What one considers essential frequently grows out of the context of personal and communal experience.

The essentials for a growing spiritual life — there are seven in this book — also arise out of human experience, the concrete experience of real life men and women; but it is experience examined in the light of religious reflection. These essentials are drawn from the wisdom of a variety of spiritual traditions, Christian and other. While my own roots are Catholic-Christian, I recognize and value the life-giving insights of other traditions. I often think of the advice once given by a holy Hindu woman to the effect that it is important for each of us to dig our own well, and to keep at the digging, until we reach water. She said we will recognize each other when we are refreshed by the water. If, however, we hop from well to well, we will never reach the source. I remain grateful that so many people persevere in their well-digging, enabling one another, by example, to finally drink the water of life.

Well-digging is an apt metaphor for the spiritual life. So is the journey, an image brought to prominence in these last decades of the twentieth century. That image, which can suggest taking inventory and securing provisions, inspired my naming *seven* essentials for ensuring a reliable pathway to the final destination.

I begin with the need for *mentors and guides.* The spiritual journey is of such import that some form of companionship, caring, intelligent, and wise, is a fundamental necessity. Practical suggestions are offered regarding where to look for this resource and what to expect from it. Subsequent chapters cast a spotlight on the other essentials: *solitude and silence, authentic community, discovering the sacred in the ordinary, savoring life's gifts, cultivating lightness and laughter,* and ultimately *surrendering to God* who is our final destination. These essentials are not remote or difficult to locate. They are available to all of us.

In many religious traditions *story* is the vehicle for revelation and understanding. I have included, therefore, a number of true stories to illustrate each essential. In addition, there are excerpts from the sacred writings of various world religions; and since

God's Holy Spirit often works through imagination, literature is an important provision in these pages.

These seven essentials are life-giving insofar as real men and women practice them, refining them for their time and culture. For that reason I hope that readers will share with me their own experiences of these seven, adding other essentials as they see fit. I, and the Crossroad Publishing Company, welcome your responses. They will enable all of us to pursue a sacred conversation about those things that matter most to us and that refresh us, as does water on a long, long journey. Your stories will help light the way for others.

SEVEN
ESSENTIALS
— *for the* —
SPIRITUAL
JOURNEY

First Essential

Mentors and Guides

On the way of wisdom I direct you,
I lead you on straightforward paths,
When you walk, your step will not be impeded,
and should you run, you will not stumble.

(Proverbs 4:11–12)

WHO OF US undertakes an important journey without a map or a guidebook of some kind? In the next few weeks I will be journeying to Rome, a city I have visited many times, occasionally for lengthy stays. Still, my green Michelin book is packed and I have spent some time each evening studying a picture guide to the churches of Rome. I'm interested in viewing the works of Caravaggio, Raphael, Titian, and others whose glorious paintings abide in small, sometimes hidden away, churches and chapels.

In addition to the valued guidebooks, I've also consulted a colleague who lived in Rome for many years, knowing that his experience can help me. I don't want to waste precious time and energy wandering through the back streets of the eternal city, charming though they are. I want to see the masterpieces, face to face, in their natural settings, and I need guidance to achieve that simple goal.

The more difficult, complex or even dangerous undertakings demand even more personal attention, namely, a hands-on guide who accompanies us step by step. The ascent of Mt. Sinai or a trek across the Egyptian desert is infinitely more secure and efficient if a strong and knowledgeable guide is by one's side.

So, too, when one enters onto the spiritual pathway, full of enthusiasm, wanting to be in ever more conscious communion with God, the pathway is not always smooth and straight. It can be "strange and wild" as the poet Dante knew. A guide or a mentor can often make all the difference in whether one gives up the journey or presses on, open to the adventures, delights, and discoveries that await. Trusted and trustworthy guides and mentors are foundational to spiritual growth. These are the men and women who have themselves traversed the spiritual path, with all its dangers, and come through victorious. Their wisdom transcends time and culture and is applicable to the concrete realities of ordinary life: the life of family and work and neighborhood, as well as the more hidden inner life. Spiritual guides are valued in all the great world religions. The Talmud, for example, is full of stories of the folly of pursuing the spiritual life without such a companion. In fact, one is advised not even to read the Jewish mystical literature until sufficiently learned in the law. This presumes a wise and compassionate rabbi close at hand.

Saints as Mentors

Saints, who are present in some form in all religious traditions, have been mentors to many. In my own tradition of Roman Catholicism I am indebted to a whole host of saints, but St. Teresa of Avila stands out, she who was largely responsible for the reform of the Carmelite order in sixteenth-century Spain. You may understandably wonder what possible relationship could a late twentieth-century American woman — wife, mother, grandmother — have with a cloistered Renaissance nun.

Many years ago as a young mother of several small children I was looking for clues about how to organize life in some centered, meaningful way. This desire for order seemed especially heightened around five in the evening, when children seem most inventive. I thought a mystic might have a few helpful ideas short of entering a monastery.

I became attracted to St. Teresa through a mothers' prayer group. The group met weekly in a home while one of the mothers cared for the preschool children at a different site. In the hour and a half of prayer we tried to learn to be attentive to the silence, to share our prayer needs aloud, to ponder whatever Scripture passage had been chosen for the day, and to locate additional spiritual resources for our continuing quest. Several of us opted for the writings of St. Teresa.

I discovered in her works a virtual guidebook for prayer and contemplation. She suggested when and how to start the practice of meditative prayer. She explained the value of formal prayers and praying aloud. She pointed out little — and big — turns in the road where prayer might become difficult or even disagreeable. She encouraged patience and endurance. A mother of small children could easily see patterns in her own life reflected in the teachings of the saint. Teresa's pithy sayings also seemed to be inerrantly on target. I especially liked "There's a time for partridge and a time for penance," which often served as a perfect 5:00 p.m. mantra of sorts. The Spanish saint gradually became part of our family.

For many years now, a reproduction of the famous Velázquez painting of St. Teresa has hung in our kitchen. In it Teresa is holding a quill pen, a symbol of her theological doctrine. (She is one of the three women "doctors" in the Roman Catholic canon. The others are Catherine of Siena and Thérèse of Lisieux.) One day my then nineteen-year-old son, home from college on what seemed to me yet another endless academic break, pointed to the portrait, and in between bites of Cheerios informed me that as a little boy he always thought St. Teresa was holding a paper airplane that was about to take off. And of course he wondered why his school frowned on similar activities from small boys.

We had a wonderful few minutes together laughing about his

misperception and gazing affectionately at St. Teresa. Only later did I realize the missed opportunity for a deeper sharing. I could have — should have — told him why Teresa was so important to me, why I kept her close at hand in the kitchen, the center of our family's life. He needs to know that this faraway nun, long gone to God, can help us navigate the inner chaos that rises up from time to time in all of us. I must look for the opportunity to do so. Numerous other saints in many different traditions are ready to share their wisdom and experience. We need only seek them out.

Thomas Kelly: A Quaker Saint

Quakers (the Society of Friends), an unstructured and non-centralized religious group, is not often thought of in terms of "saints." Yet this spiritual tradition, that emphasizes the inner light which each one of us bears, has produced its own pantheon of spiritually developed men and women whose knowledge of the inner life is itself life-giving. Thomas Kelly, an American, is one.

A friend of mine, a professor of history whose whole adult life has been in academia, recently wrote to me of her yearly reading of Thomas Kelly's small book, *Testament of Devotion*. Kelly, a devout Quaker, who died in 1941 at the age of forty-seven, was also an academic, so they have that specific affinity. About her annual "read" she wrote as follows:

> The writing alone does not explain the power of this book. Its content is vital. Here is an explication of Christian life in all its simplicity and power. As a Quaker Kelly is unfettered by an elaborate theology or anthropology. He begins and ends with Quakerism's central tenant — the indwelling of the Light in each person. Once accepted, one is asked only *to live as if such belief were true*. The command to the believer is to practice the presence of God by a continual

turning through prayer and adoration to that inner Light. In so doing the Christian becomes a witness whose life is a testament not of belief or morality but of devotion. Such a life is characterized by a passion for personal holiness and a sense of utter humility. By giving all, one gains all. The way is through the full, complete, and perpetual return of the soul to the inner sanctuary where one finds God. It is, for me, an urgent invitation to love more deeply. That's why I read it every year.

My friend, while drawn to Kelly's intellectual honesty and interest in Eastern religions, is most affected by his direct experience of the Divine Presence, which he later described to some friends as having been literally melted down by the love of God.[1] His spiritual depth is evident in his words to a 1938 Friends' Meeting:

> To you in this room who are seekers, to you, young and old who have toiled all night and caught nothing, but who want to launch out into the deeps and let down your nets for a draught...there is a resting place of absolute peace and joy and power and radiance and security. There is a divine Center into which your life can slip, a new and absolute orientation in God, a Center where you live with Him and out of which you see all of life, through new and radiant vision, tinged with new sorrows and pangs, new joys unspeakable and full of glory.[2]

This is the man whom my friend turns to over and over again.

Douglas Steere, himself a respected Quaker teacher of the spiritual life and a person I was privileged to know in an ecumenical spirituality group, points out that Kelly developed from a man with "knowledge about" God to one with an "unmistakable acquaintance with [God]."[3]

There is a difference. And it is that difference that one should look for in a guide. Sometimes such a one is quite near at hand, in the guise of familiarity.

Pastors: Mentors of the Soul

In the early 1960s Arlington County (where I live) was holding on to the last vestiges of institutional segregation, present even in churches, but more by custom and housing patterns. The Catholic parish I attended was settled into such a pattern. Virginia traditions were highly valued; change seemed unduly upsetting. Not everyone, however, was content with the status quo. Some of us who came from other parts of the country or who had been reading Martin Luther King, Jr., and John LaFarge, S.J., wanted to be more pro-active. The Catholic Interracial Council seemed a safe starting place to initiate some beginning discussion. But when I tried to arrange a parish program on the topic of integration I was cautioned to "slow down." Being young, energetic, and willful I was not at all ready to take that suggestion. I wanted help in organizing for change!

Someone who knew the inner workings of Arlington suggested I talk with Fr. David Ray, who pastored a small mission church in south Arlington, in an African-American community, one clearly segregated. "He's a priest who knows how to get things done," I was told.

So one autumn night in 1963 I rang his doorbell, having called ahead for an appointment. As I waited for some response, bits of television newscasts flashed through my mind with vivid images of students of both races riding into the South, ready to offer up their safety for *everyone's* right to vote. I felt caught between the inhumanity we all were witnessing via modern communications and my own anxiety at standing on a strange doorstep in a strange neighborhood. My knees were shaking as I promised myself that in the future I would stay home where I belonged with my husband and four very young children. I almost cried aloud, "What am I doing here?" when the door opened. There stood the man I presumed to be Fr. Ray, "the civil rights priest." He was wearing a cassock and was reading aloud from a book of Langston Hughes's poetry. He didn't greet me — or say anything, really — he just kept reading poetry, beckoning me to follow him. The rectory living room was stacked with books, magazines, and newspapers. I had to move some of them to sit down.

When the poetry reading was finished (for the moment) I hurriedly described my problem and asked for guidance. What I expected was that he would point me in the direction of some kind of community organizing workshop. Maybe even arrange for one.

Instead, with perfect confidence, he said that it was essential that I read and ponder the works of Evelyn Underhill. I had no idea who this person was. Fr. Ray told me she was English, an Anglican lay woman, a spiritual writer — and he thought I needed to read her very carefully. Of course, he talked too about the cultural-social burdens which African-Americans bore, but he kept coming back to Underhill. I left the rectory in a somewhat disoriented state, but also more focused than when I arrived. Driving home I began to wonder about the charisms pastors might have in regard to floundering souls in need of a compass.

Evelyn Underhill: An Everyday Mystic

The next day I headed for the public library in search of Evelyn Underhill and felt a profound relief to discover a few of her books on the library shelves. It seems odd to recall that in 1963 books on the spiritual life were not in abundance as they are now. I came home with a copy of *Practical Mysticism* and determined never to be without it, so directly did it speak to me. That trip to the library began a most wonderful relationship with Underhill, one that has lasted for decades. Over the years I hunted in used book stores and wrote to English publishing companies in search of her books which were not readily available. That has changed thanks to the unflagging scholarship of Dr. Dana Greene, who has edited many of Underhill's essays and journals and produced an outstanding biography of this inspiring writer.[4]

Practical Mysticism, though, is the book I go back to over and over again, ever since the day in 1963 when I read there, "Mysticism is the art of union with Reality."[5] Bedrock reality was what I wanted. I believed Underhill when she wrote that this definition was inclusive of philosophers and visionaries and suitable for poets and for saints, indeed suitable for everyone, even ordinary citizens of the earthly city. Furthermore, she believed it was not only suitable, but open to all. This seemed to promise endless possibilities. What is needed, she insisted, is a retraining of consciousness, a cleansing of our ordinary habits of perception. Retraining starts with what she calls "self-simplification." She reminds her readers of moments of involuntary contemplation: sudden happenings when you lose yourself in a swift and satisfying experience.[6] I think of the first time I heard Vladimir Horowitz's rendering of Schuman's "Traumerie," or the many times I've watched Canada geese take off in ordered formation, or the moment I saw my firstborn child. These were moments of perfect coherence.

Underhill's insistence, however, that one need not be content with these transient moments of unity held out a new kind of hope. One could pass into such a world by a willingness to expend effort and commitment, a reeducation of sorts. What this new education involves is simplification, simplification of our attention, our affections, and our will. Through it all weaves the thread of discipline. And from it all we become artists of human life. Therein lies the great practicality of mysticism.

Over time I came to realize that for me the works of Evelyn Underhill were like water in the desert. I came to see that what Fr. Ray gave me the first night we met was the best he had, namely, that which had shaped his own work for racial justice. He told me, in effect, that unless I was serious about soul work, everything else I was trying to do would be built on shifting sand. It was years before I understood why he greeted me with verses from Langston Hughes and kept repeating one line, "My soul has grown deep like the rivers."[7] He wanted my soul to become that deep.

Domestic Guides: Grandmothers

Sometimes the needed guide is within the family circle. Grandmothers, with the dual strength of closeness and distance, fulfill that role in many cultures. In many Latin traditions grandmothers are a decisive formative influence on children at all stages. And, too, in the African-American culture. Who can ever forget young Ruby Bridges's reply to a national guardsman who was escorting her into the recently desegregated Louisiana school in the 1960s? The guardsman, who had been in field battle overseas, said he had never seen such courage as this tiny six-year-old displayed in the face of unadulterated hatred. Ruby told the guardsman that she just did what her Granny told her: she kept on praying.

I regularly see Vietnamese grandmothers instructing their young granddaughters in Catholic ritual. These are gentle lessons at weekday Mass; older women and children smiling at one another as children learn the ways of ritual and worship.

Ruth, a Catholic wife, mother, grandmother, and now a great-grandmother, with a recent advanced theology degree and a lifelong passion for social justice, credits her grandmother, Hildegard, with engendering in her the belief that God's gifts to us are to be used to help others.

Ruth lived with her grandparents from age seven to ten while her parents were trying to establish a business in West Virginia. Those years are viewed by Ruth as a precious time of spiritual formation in her life. She observed her grandmother fully engaged with her own gifts — music (she taught piano more for love than for money), herbal medicine and healing arts, and a deep religious sensibility — and sharing them with others. She imparted to Ruth an abiding sense that women have the capacity to shape lives of creativity and service that are enriching to the wider community as well as personally satisfying to them.

Hildegard's artistic nature was reflected in her piety. Jesus crucified was vividly present to her first as a human being enveloped in blood, tears, and unspeakable suffering. His divinity did nothing to diminish the pain that Hildegard saw in her dominant image of Jesus. Even as a young child Ruth was deeply affected by her grandmother's sense that Jesus' suffering was to be found way beyond the confines of Palestine.

One spring day while playing in her grandmother's garden, Ruth became intensely aware of the flowering plant known as "bleeding hearts." In her mind's eye the bleeding hearts were transformed into the dying Jesus. Deep in her spirit she heard the words she believes to this day came from some divine source, "I'm crying over the whole world."

Ruth carried those words with her into adulthood and explicitly connects that experience with her abiding and active concern for social justice. She has marched and held prayer vigils for civil rights, for peace and justice in Vietnam, and for a domestic agenda that acknowledges the human dignity of the poor and their needs. In her sixties she took a graduate degree in theology to help her articulate the spiritual truth that had been growing in her since childhood. Now in her seventies, and somewhat slowed by arthritis, Ruth continues her spiritual journey, with her husband, following the rule of St. Francis. Even while joyfully engaged with their six children, thirteen grandchildren, and recently a great-grandchild, they offer endless hospitality to friends from many different cultures. Through good times and bad, sickness and health, Ruth has remained faithful to her understanding that social activism is like water for the thirsting Jesus upon the cross. Marches and White House demonstrations are not possible for her these days, but telephones and letters continue to relay her consistent message that those in power who ignore the demands of justice and the impulses of mercy put our society in jeopardy. She still regards grandmother Hildegard as her principal mentor.

Spiritual Direction: A Special Form of Friendship

One of the most ancient forms of spiritual guidance and one that is having a major renaissance is that of spiritual direction. In a one-on-one relationship, the spiritual director listens with love, the love of the Holy Spirit, to the other (the directee), who shares an account of his or her journey toward a fuller life in God. The one who seeks spiritual direction often relates the struggles and the secrets of the soul in faltering or disguised language. This is understandable: soul language is not characterized by glibness. The spiritual director, however, is committed to the deepest, most generous form of listening, a listening so deep that the light, guidance, strength, and consolation of God's Holy Spirit are given ample room.

> To live with the Spirit of God is to be a listener.
> It is to keep the vigil of mystery,
> earthless and still.
> One leans to catch the stirring of the Spirit,
> strange as the wind's will.[8]

This more conscious life in the Spirit does not occur all at once. Like all good exercises, consistency is vitally important.

Meetings might be monthly or bimonthly — or weekly if one's inner life is particularly active. The point is that consistency will improve the health of the soul, just as consistent exercise improves the health of the body.

Interest in spiritual direction has grown noticeably in the last twenty years. There had been an assumption that this form of guidance was principally for Catholics, and most likely monks and nuns or those in a crisis situation. But as knowledge about spirituality has moved from the margins to the center of intentional religious life, ordinary men and women from different religious traditions are seeking out competent directors.

And who are these directors? In the early days of Christianity they were the hermits of the desert — the spiritual fathers and mothers — who sought the face of God in solitude and silence. Other serious seekers searched them out, staying nearby to observe and to imitate. They would ask questions of the father or mother about whether a particular practice was leading to God or not, and the more experienced man or woman would render an opinion.

Over time the desert gave way to monasteries and to other forms of religious organization. Those considering life apart from the ordinary dynamics of worldly commerce, and those actually living out such commitments, were deemed in need of spiritual direction, and the directors were men and women of their own number. Occasionally, anchorites were consulted — Lady Julian of Norwich is one well-known example — and occasionally ordinary people (pilgrims, for example) sought their guidance. But generally speaking, spiritual directors came from the ranks of the ordained, and their guidance was for those in consecrated vows.

All that has changed. Now large numbers of laity who have no intention of entering a monastery meet regularly with spiritual directors. Furthermore, the director may just as likely be a lay woman or man, with the greater number being women.

"RN" is a good example. Her spiritual ministry began in the mid-1960s with the mothers' prayer group described earlier. In time, the prayer group experience led RN to some ecumenical adult religious education work and was followed by systematic study with a national institute devoted to spiritual growth, including spiritual direction. Immersion in a Jesuit parish introduced her more fully to the Spiritual Exercises of St. Ignatius. This development in her life was not intentionally planned; rather it has consisted of following faithfully, step by step, the leadings of the Spirit. Over time others sought her help as they tried to navigate their own inner pathways. Today, RN is spiritual director to twenty people, some of whom are men, a few of whom are priests. Her directees include religious leaders with national responsibilities.[9]

The question remains: How does one locate a skilled and willing spiritual director?

There is a quiet debate over whether or not a director should be "professionally" trained, a debate fueled not only by the demand and real need, but also by the proliferation of various spiritual guidance training programs. These programs are generally well thought out and offer support and critique for those actively engaged in this special ministry. Ministers from religious traditions other than Catholic find them particularly useful. Kenneth Leech, an Anglican spiritual guide and writer, argues for another point of view, however.

I stand by my insistence in 1977 that spiritual direction is not essentially a ministry for specialists and professionals, but part of the ordinary pastoral ministry of every parish and every Christian community. Even more so do I stand by my suggestion that the role of "training" is extremely limited, and that this ministry is essentially a by-product of a life of prayer and growth in holiness.[10]

Other experienced spiritual directors fall somewhere in the middle. John Crossin, an Oblate of St. Francis de Sales, tends to situate spiritual direction in the context of spiritual friendship. Still, he believes that some level of training can assist in evaluating the occasional person who seems to be having extraordinary spiritual experiences. Most important for Crossin is that the director be rooted in the teaching of his or her church as a corrective to subjectivism. Quoting St. Francis de Sales, he says that the director should be filled with charity, learning, and prudence.[11]

For twenty years I have been blessed with both the spiritual direction and the spiritual friendship of a Benedictine monk, a relationship that began between two strangers. I sought help in being faithful to my own rule of prayer and guidance concerning an ever-widening arc of human relationships. At first — for several years, in fact — I knew nothing of this monk's personal life story. In truth, I wanted and needed a very clear focus. The process of disclosure and response began to elicit from me something original and free, some center of creativity only previously hinted at. It was not something I observed as it was unfolding; only in retrospect could I name the movements of the Spirit.

Over time, as trust deepened, what began as somewhat utilitarian on my part, took the shape of friendship. Aelred of Rievaulx best describes it: "Your friend is the companion of your soul ... from whom you hide nothing, from whom you fear nothing."[12] I am acutely aware of how my soul friend/director has evoked my own originality, especially when I have buried it in a mountain of trivia. I'm sure he has this effect on others as well, for so strong and stable is his own spiritual core that the essence of an issue quickly emerges.

Through our exchanges I have come to appreciate my particular vocation, one lived in a web of relationships with family and friends, with my church community, and with ecumenical colleagues. Our meetings release in me a sense of gratitude for the richness of my own life even with its particular failures and suffering. I continue to learn about the folly of trying to control the future. My wise monk reminds me, over and over again, that the troubles of the day are sufficient unto themselves, and that it is best for all of us to practice living in the present moment. That brings me face to face with the Reality which Evelyn Underhill understood so well and which is at the heart of the Benedictine tradition of spiritual formation rooted in friendship.

The Ignatian Way: Spiritual Exercises

Iñigo López de Loyola, known to history as Ignatius of Loyola, founder of the Jesuits, was born in the Basque country, at a time when Europe was entering the great era of exploration. For Ignatius, the exploration would be in the inward regions of the soul. His story is well known, and the details of his biography readily available.[13]

The method of spiritual direction or guidance known as the Spiritual Exercises grew out of his own experiences. A profound illumination occurred while he was engaged in the life of a poor pilgrim. Walking along a river bank he found himself immersed in God. According to Jesuit writer Joseph Tetlow, Ignatius grasped that God's plan is really a project that each person on earth contributes to; what God *hopes* in us rises in our consciousness and, by God's grace, to free enactment.[14] The steps in Ignatius's own journey to God, and their application to his first followers, comprise the heart of the book known as the *Spiritual Exercises*, which has been in constant use for 450 years. What is offered therein is a structured religious experience, not speculative theological hypotheses.

The Exercises may be undertaken in several ways with a spiritual director who may or may not be a Jesuit. The classic method is the "thirty-day retreat," where one withdraws from all activity and enters into deep silence in a retreat house. It is a time of intense prayer and meditation on the Scriptures assigned by the director, who is consulted daily or every other day. The experience of the daily prayer is discussed, how desires and decisions are emerging, and what feelings and emotions are surfacing. This is not the same as confession or therapy, but is directly related to the immediacy of prayer and meditation. Tetlow points out that in the Jesuit historical tradition one need not be Catholic to undertake the Spiritual Exercises.[15]

Few people today (or in any period) have the luxury of thirty days apart in a country retreat. Ignatius knew this to be true in his own time and so devised a method whereby men and women could experience the Exercises while continuing with their work and domestic obligations. According to this method, known as "The 19th Annotation," the person commits to an hour and a half of prayer a day, plus regular meetings with the spiritual director, weekly or biweekly. The at-home retreatants may arrange the hour and half of daily prayer in a number of ways. Perhaps an hour of prayer in the morning, and a half-hour at night. The director may suggest other arrangements according to the person's duties. In any case, the same structure as the thirty-day retreat is followed, that is, scriptural meditations and contemplations. Other resources, poetry for example, may also be utilized. As in the longer retreat the person will traverse through awareness of God's mercy and humanity's sin, Jesus' entry into human history, including his public life and ministry, his suffering and death and his resurrection, and his continuing life in the world. Desolations and consolations will be noted and examined.

The "19th Annotation" is growing in popularity. Some Jesuit parishes are training gifted lay people to undertake this rather specialized ministry. I have found that young adults, especially those who have had a deep experience of mission among the poor, are looking for some reliable resource to help them discern the next steps in their lives. Discernment and decision are central to this form of spiritual direction. Historically, one undertook the Spiritual Exercises precisely to make a decision according to God's will about which life path to choose.

I recently spoke with a young woman, a graduate of a Catholic university who completed two and a half years in a Honduran mission and is trying to decide whether to apply to medical school. Her wrestling is truly soul-deep, and I feel sure the Exercises could help with her decision.

True Guides: The Way of Truth

Authentic mentors and guides share with us what they know about ultimate truth and elicit from us a commitment to live our lives in absolute respect for the truth. They are found not only near at hand in our parishes and families, in monasteries and universities, but sometimes they are in the most unlikely places.

Some years ago I read a book which vividly illustrates that point, Eugenia Ginzburg's account of her eighteen years of exile in Siberia, *Within the Whirlwind.*

Ginzburg was a communist intellectual, married with two small sons, when she was caught up in the 1937 Stalinist purge. For eighteen long years she was moved from camp to camp, working in kitchens, on farms, in tree nurseries, and in hospitals. It was in a Siberian hospital that she met Anton Walter, a German-Catholic homeopathic physician who later became her second husband. Their love for one another, and her love for poetry, the language of the soul, sustained her throughout the whirlwind of those prison years. Eugenia and Anton become partners in the truest sense of the term, interdependent and complementary. In the midst of degradation and deprivation not only did they survive, they thrived. Anton, who was a devout Catholic, became a spiritual mentor for Eugenia, who was without religion. She de-

scribed one of their earliest meetings. Anton was performing an
autopsy while she took notes.

"And where is the immortal soul," I said pensively when the
processing was finished. The doctor raised his eyes and gave
me a close look. He became unusually serious. "It's a good
thing you're asking yourself the question. It would be a bad
thing if you imagined the immortal soul were necessarily
located in one of the imperfect organs of our body."[16]

She accepted this from the man she came to call the jolly
saint. When her memoir was published (after her release from
prison but smuggled out of Moscow) it was greeted the world
over with acclaim. She interpreted the praise this way:

It was perfectly clear to me that I owed this not to any special literary merit in the book but solely to its truthfulness.
People who have been totally starved of the simple un-
sophisticated truth were grateful to anyone who would take
the trouble of telling them, *de profundis*, how it really was.[17]

She went on to assure her readers that she had written nothing but the truth while acknowledging that there might be
inaccuracies about dates or specific incidents. Her point was that
there are no lies in the book, no politically correct sophisms, no
deliberate exclusions. She added that at her age there was no
point at all in making things up. Finally, she admitted that she
had not written down the whole truth because no one knows the
whole truth. But she was sure that she had written nothing but
the truth. Anton had long ago pointed the way.

Spiritual guides and mentors enable us to humbly acknowledge
that while we can never know the whole truth about a situation (or even about ourselves), we are free to choose the way of
truthfulness, over and over again.

Practical Suggestions

The question naturally arises regarding how to recognize or find a spiritual guide or mentor.

Look around your ordinary environment. Mentors often simply rise up in the midst of our everyday lives. I remember a friend who endured a difficult career move from one government agency to the Pentagon, where he thought he would simply have to endure his time until retirement. How surprised he was to discover that his immediate supervisor was a man of profound faith who began each day seeking divine guidance, who made frequent visits to the chapel, who read and reflected on a whole range of social ethics. My friend saw in him a confidant with whom he could discuss his occasional qualms of conscience about governmental policy, but also someone with whom he could share questions of ultimate concern. Most of all, this person modeled for my friend how one could be a man of religious conviction, internal integrity, and professional competence, which made my friend's final years of government service ones of personal learning and growth.

Make inquiries. Often simply asking questions about who might be a good spiritual guide can yield a treasure of information. This is especially true if our friends or networks of acquaintances share our spiritual interests. Sometimes a good friend will simply offer a suggestion. That is how I met my Benedictine spiritual friend.

Ruth, whom you met earlier in this chapter, knew I was in need of a spiritual director. I had had the blessing of that kind of spiritual relationship before, but for several years was without a personal director. Ruth called me at my office one day to say she had found a spiritual director for me. "He's a monk at the nearby abbey," she said, "steeped in Scripture and literature; you can give something to each other." She had gone on a retreat which he led.

Trusting Ruth's intuitive sense and her knowledge of me, I followed through. I called the abbey, located the monk, set up a one-time meeting to see if there were possibilities, and I have been grateful forever after.

Go on a retreat. Ruth found my spiritual director and soul friend at *her* retreat, but others discover the possibility of guidance when they attend a retreat. The retreat leader is very visible, soul exposed, and we can often ascertain if *this* person is one to whom we can entrust the next steps of our spiritual journey. So a retreat house, and especially a personally experienced retreat, is a good place to begin the search. And, of course, retreat houses that specialize in Ignatian retreats are superb resources for locating a director skilled in the Spiritual Exercises of St. Ignatius.

Be attentive to your church environment. A person who is on an intentional spiritual journey, who is serious about spiritual growth, will begin to observe the men and women who inhabit the immediate environment. You may sense in your parish priest or pastoral worker someone skilled in the intricacies of the soul. You may be drawn to a neighbor or a member of a prayer group or study group because you sense in that person what St. Teresa called toughness of mind and gentleness of spirit, essentials in her view for spiritual direction. You may want to meet one or two times with the person to test the rightness of your instincts.

Consult the Scriptures. One of the great biblical stories of guidance is that of the archangel Raphael in the Book of Tobit. Raphael guides the young man Tobias to a life of safety and love, and does so in the form of friendship. When he finally reveals his true identity, he reiterates the common angelic imperative: Be not afraid. That is what mentors and guides typically do for us. They help us to proceed on our way, unhampered by fear. Look for scriptural courage, trust, and leadings.

Second Essential

SOLITUDE AND SILENCE

*When you pray, go to your inner room, close the door, and pray
to your Father in secret.*   (MATTHEW 6:6)

LIFE GROWS IN AND OUT of stark solitude. This is something farmers know when they plant seeds that will remain
for months in darkness, unseen. This is something that parents
know, too, as they wait for the birth of a child who develops in
secret. This is something that each man and woman knows who
is growing in consciousness of his or her essential being.[18] It is
something at the heart of religious experience.

Certainly artists of all kinds know how essential solitude is to
their work. May Sarton, poet, novelist, and writer of journals,
deliberately chose a life alone where her consciousness could be
honed in such a way as to heighten the vividness of human experience. Friends came and went in her life — and were important
to her, certainly — but she rejoiced when she could take up her
real life again, "time alone to explore what is happening or has
happened. Without the interruptions, nourishing and madden-
ing, this life would become arid. Yet I taste it fully only when I
am alone here and the house and I resume old conversations,"
she wrote in her journal.[19]

Carmelite poet Jessica Powers had a similar appreciation of
solitude, and it was undoubtedly a factor in her decision to enter
a Carmelite monastery in 1941. This was the period when she
was receiving critical acclaim for her work. Her first book of
poems had been published. The future was wide open before her.

Instead she entered one of the most rigorous religious orders, one where nuns spend a considerable amount of time alone. In many ways it was the perfect setting for her to become ever more her contemplative, poetic self, the self who ceaselessly sought God. For forty-seven years, in deepest solitude and silence, she continued to explore the mysteries of the human soul and the mysteries of God, fashioning a wealth of poetry out of her discoveries. Her language is so true and uncontrived that one senses it is directly related to the silence in which it germinated. She wrote these lines after a decade in the cloister:

COUNSEL FOR SILENCE

Go without ceremony of departure
and shade no subtlest word with your farewell.
Let the air speak the mystery of your absence,
and the discerning have their minor feast
on savory possible or probable.
Seeing the body present, they will wonder
where went the secret soul, by then secure
out past your grief beside some torrent's pure
refreshment. Do not wait to copy down
the name, much less the address, of who might need you.
Here you are pilgrim with no ties of earth.
Walk out alone and make the never-told
your healing distance and your household.
And let the ravens feed you.[20]

For all of us who desire to become artful human beings, in touch with the creative dimensions of our family life, our work, our friendships, and in touch with the mystery of God, solitude is also an essential condition. Alone and apart, in periods of regular solitude interspersed in the daily, weekly, and monthly activities of our busy lives, we can scrape away the accretions that clutter up our interior and exterior space. We can come to the simplicity expressed in Jessica Powers's verse, a simplicity which cuts through surface clutter.

Modern life does not readily support such an idea, however. People tend to live at some distance from their work places, and that requires many hours of commuting. The result is little time for parents to be with their children or with one another, and so any discretionary time that appears is generally used for family activities. Contemporary architecture is also a factor. Houses constructed after World War II feature great open spaces, with kitchen and living space and dining area all blending together. Small secluded studies, libraries, or just hidden nooks and crannies are rare indeed.[21] How then can we find the time and space for solitude and for the primary phenomenon of silence? And how important is it?

Who doubts that we live in a noise-filled world? Radio and television have long been integrated in our culture, but add to that headphones, talking trains, musical computers, Muzak everywhere (including supermarkets), cell phones, fax machines, and talking elevators, and one sees how rare, indeed, are solitude and silence. Even the sound of those words — silence and solitude — carries a certain mystery. Yet, silence is the seedbed of the creative life, a preparation for utterance or action. This is vividly illustrated in the lives of many religious leaders.

The prophet Elijah, in his impassioned search for God, believed he would find the Holy One on Mt. Horeb (1 Kings 19:11–13). A variety of natural phenomena surrounded Elijah. At first he thinks God may be encountered in the earthquake. Not so. Then a great wind sweeps the mountain. God is not there, either. And God is not in the fire that follows. It is not until Elijah enters the cave, the silent cave, that he knows the presence of the living God. The Presence is manifested in the center of stillness, in the barest of whispers. The encounter strengthens Elijah to continue on his mission to bring the Israelites back to their God.

Jesus, too, knew the power of silence. He tried to get his followers to look for the still point within their own persons. "The Kingdom of God is within you," he insisted. He also set an example, going apart from time to time, to be alone and silent with the God he called his Father. The solitude refreshed him for his ministry of teaching and healing.

Thich Nhat Hanh, a Vietnamese Buddhist monk who teaches the way of mindfulness, writes that we are entirely capable of touching the ultimate dimension. "When we touch one thing with deep awareness," he says, "we touch everything."[22] In this he echoes Evelyn Underhill, who believed that our consciousness can be trained, or retrained, to apprehend the depths of Reality, what Thich Nhat Hanh calls the ultimate dimension. The issue is not the value of silence and solitude — all religions respect that value — but how to make these rhythms part of everyday life. One way is to seek a different environment from time to time.

Places Apart

The simple white chapel at Holy Cross Abbey in Berryville, Virginia, is steeped in silence. There is a texture to it, and sitting there one feels surrounded by solid reality (although "solid" is not exactly the right term). When the Trappist monks enter, dressed in the ancient black and white habits of their order, the silence holds, and even deepens. The monks bow deeply, a gesture of infinite care. When they chant the psalms or say the prayers of the Mass or read the Scriptures aloud, every word, every syllable is weighted, like stones dropping into a still, clear pond.

Today, the monastic silence reaches out to ordinary people, lawyers and teachers, artists and farmers who come to the monastery to partake of the fruitfulness of the silent life. They may come for as much as a week's retreat or as little as a day of quiet prayer or attendance at vespers.

One artist, a painter of contemporary icons, says her heart grows larger when she breathes in the silence of the place; a side effect is new energy for her work. A business leader feels less frantic and grasping after only a day walking the monastery paths and sitting in the chapel. He brings the monastery peace to his work and to his family.

Trappists no longer keep the strict silence which was associated with their way of life for centuries and which added a touch of wonder to them. It used to be they never spoke, except for prayer, study, spiritual direction, or whatever was necessary for their dedicated life. There was no casual conversation. Over time they developed a particular sign language which enabled them to live their common life with some degree of efficiency. Today they may speak, and they do; but still, there is no frivolous talk, no radio blaring, no sound but the wind in the trees and the human voice in ancient chant. The atmosphere is one of clarity.

The openness of Trappist monasteries is a development of the last thirty years. Monastic communities began to realize that while their hidden, quiet life had always affected the larger world (after all, everything is connected according to one of the primary laws of physics), some more direct sharing could help feed the hunger they sensed in the lives of busy men and women. Many monasteries established guest houses for private retreats. Monastic communities welcomed their neighbors to Sunday Mass and daily prayer. People of all faiths have sought and received guidance in their prayer. One particular form has had an enormous impact.

Centering Prayer: An Entrance to Silence

St. Joseph's Trappist monastery in Spencer, Massachusetts, released a stream of prayer in which countless men and women, lay people as well as nuns and monks, have entered. It is centering prayer, the reappropriation of ancient meditation, in which one word guides the pray-er into the silence of God. The word is taken from the Scriptures, a word from God as it were, which serves as an anchor to hold one in the Presence in a way that transcends all our powers of intellect and language.[23] For many years retreats devoted to learning this particular prayer form have been available, guided by competent monastic teachers. A network of people who practice centering prayer supports those on this spiritual pathway.[24]

Dom John Main, O.S.B., one of the best-known teachers in this particular prayer form, is clear that we must have the courage to become more and more silent to truly enter into the experience of centering prayer. He doesn't minimize the difficulty involved. He points out that this is not just a matter of keeping our tongues still, but of achieving a state of alert stillness in our mind and heart, a state of consciousness unfamiliar to most Westerners. He writes that the task of meditation is to bring our chattering, distracted minds to stillness, silence, and concentration, which he names as "proper service," the aim given us by the psalmist: "Be still and know that I am God."[25] This form of prayer is in no way a reinforcement of ego or narcissism. Rather, according to Main, it is participation in the mission of Christ as he himself stated it: "I have come that you may have life, and have it in all its fullness" (John 10:10). Silence and meditation are about the fullness of life, about discovering the true self where, according to Richard of St. Victor, the divine light begins to shine through.[26] Who would not be warmed by such a light?

Inside Silence

Karl Rahner, S.J., one of the most influential theologians of the twentieth century, has given a profoundly personal account of his own prayer in the atmosphere of silence. Unlike centering prayer, which is essentially wordless, Rahner's encounters with silence are more like pouring out his soul to God, much like the great figures of Hebrew Scriptures. He laments his attachment to daily routine:

> My soul is crammed full, from top to bottom with the trite, the commonplace, the insignificant, the routine.... What will become of me, dear God, if my life goes on like this? How will I feel at the hour of my death? Then there will be no more "daily routine"; then I shall suddenly be abandoned by all the things that now fill up my days here on earth.[27]

Rahner is realist enough to know that becoming a hermit will not solve his problem. He acknowledges to God, his silent God, that any path on which he can approach the Divine must lead right through "the very middle of my ordinary life."[28] He finds his ordinary life is filled with love for all those who have enriched him: family, friends, and colleagues. He feels them to be with him, especially those who have died. They are there in the silence that surrounds God and him. He says to God about these departed ones, "Their silence is their loudest call to me because it is the echo of Your silence.... Their voice speaks in unison with You.... Their voice and Yours strive to enwrap us and all our words in Your eternal silence."[29]

In truth, Rahner's sacred conversation with the divine silence leads to the same point at which John Main and practitioners of centering prayer arrive: the still point, the *now*. It seems that whatever way one enters the silence — with a single word, with a stream of confession and complaint — a bright light awaits. A new life, as well.

Experiments with Silence

I recently heard about one man's experiment with silence. He was not searching for a prayer-path, at least not consciously, but for entry into what he sensed would be a dimension of reality not readily available in our culture. He decided not to speak on Sundays, a decision difficult to implement.

At first he avoided friends and family on Sundays. How could he explain to them that he was keeping silent for one day a week? After a while, however, total avoidance became impossible. On speaking days he told them of his need to experiment with this different way of being in the world. Gradually, people in his life-circle accepted his odd behavior.

He was not married at the time, and one Sunday a friend arranged a blind date for him. One can imagine the challenge that not speaking presented to both parties. Surprisingly, the woman was interested in his quiet experiment, and apparently understood his need to abstain from speech. They eventually married, and today both of them share in the practice of silent Sundays.

More than half a century ago Max Picard held up the almost absolute importance of silence in a world filled with meaningless sounds and self-important speech. "We live between the world of silence from which we come (creation) and the world of the other silence to which we go (death)."[30] To be in touch with reality, then, requires that we taste of silence. Picard is especially concerned about the "noise of words," that is, those words which come from other words, and not from silence. They have none of the authenticity of a primary language.

An experiment like silent Sundays, or the steadiness of Trappist life, or the silence of a Carmelite cloister can heighten the difference between noisy words and true language. In these cases the spiritual connection with language is reestablished.

Silence is a frequently overlooked element in the culture of contemporary ministry, which claims a spiritual foundation. Yet it is often that which is needed most in areas of healing.

When terrorist bombs killed a large number of Israelis who happened to live in the same neighborhood of Jerusalem, news agencies reported that the grief was so overwhelming that one rabbi said, "There is nothing we can do but sit silently with the families like the friends of Job did long ago." In the prologue to the story of Job we read that his friends decided to visit him with comfort for his many losses. But as they drew nearer to him they saw such misery that for seven days and seven nights they simply sat beside him on the ground, and the Scriptures say, "None of them said a word to him." Sometimes only silence will do.

And yet, as one of French novelist Jean Sulivan's characters observes, "What we need to do is create relationships out of our deepest selves; in this way words would be born that would be true gestures of love."[31] That is the challenge for ministry, to use words in order to create or deepen relationships. It is also the challenge for all those who hold or seek a public platform and who use words to achieve their ends.

One of the reasons I was attracted to the poetry of Jessica Powers is that I found her words — simple, unadorned, direct, surprising, and spacious — to be bearers of truth, beauty, and love. There is no pretension or manipulation in her expression. She loved language and refused to violate it, rejecting what she sensed was a growing cynicism in poetry.[32] Her life in Carmel refined these basic instincts and refined the instruments of her perceptive sensibilities. Beauty and truth were nurtured in the silence of Carmel, but not without effort. We see this in her poem about hushing one's house, the symbol of the self:

> The house must first of all accept the night.
> Let it erase the walls and their display,
> impoverish the rooms till they are filled

with humble silences; let clocks be stilled
and all the selfish urgencies of day.[33]

Humble silences depend on our stilling the clocks and elimi-
nating calendars and schedules. So does the health of our souls.
And yet we resist. This is often a case of St. Paul's problem,
namely, not doing the good I want (Rom. 7:15). Sometimes we
simply do not know how to structure solitude and silence into a
busy life, full of responsibilities. It may take a crisis to overcome
reluctance. It was so in my own life.

When I was a young wife with two children under the age
of two, I contracted rheumatic fever. My doctor insisted on total
rest. He sent me first to Georgetown University Hospital for three
weeks, and then home for several more weeks of bed rest. The
babies went to New York City during this period to be cared for
by their grandparents. My husband was at his job every day. Being new to the Washington area we had few friends as yet. There
was no television at home for distraction. I had nothing to do,
lying in bed, but read Elizabethan plays (which I hadn't done
since I left teaching) and think. What I thought about was this:
I want to know God. *Know* God, directly. I want to learn to pray.
I thought about silence during that time and wondered how I
could learn to listen to the silence which I sensed surrounded
God, and which now constituted my environment.

I now realize that in fact I had answered the question which
Jesus always put to those who sought his healing, namely, what
do you want? The illness was the entrance into the experience of
solitude, silence, and prayer.

The children were permitted to return home on the condition that I would rest every afternoon for two hours. It was not
necessary that I sleep, only rest. They were to be safely "hidden
away" to nap, or not. I was told to mentally lock out everything,
including children's complaints. They soon fell into the routine

of a long afternoon nap, and I took up the practice of spiritual reading, meditation, and silent time.

With the return to health and the birth of two more children, I found the practice of solitude, undertaken because of medical necessity, had now become a spiritual necessity. A block of time apart each weekday was sacred time, as important to my total well-being as food, water, and friends.

Eventually I returned to the world of outside work: to teaching, to television production, to writing, and to administrative work at the National Conference of Catholic Bishops. Life outside the home presented the challenge of how to sustain a practice of solitude that seemed to fit into an at-home lifestyle. Once again, an unexpected intervention occurred.

I heard of a newly formed contemplative prayer group, ecumenical in composition, with clergy and laity committed to two hours of shared silence and meditation once a week. For many years that group experience of shared silence fed my interior life. Through all that time there was limited verbal exchange, usually on the part of the leadership to help us be more attentive. But it was principally our silent presence with one another that gave support to our other efforts to include a rhythm of solitude in our daily lives.[34]

The Church and Solitude

In truth most of us need help to claim nonproductive time and quiet space for ourselves. The church, with its inheritance of sabbath time, can be of enormous help. The problem, however, is that active ministry often dominates a particular church's vision of how to be an agent for God in the world. Years ago I heard the eminent French theologian Yves Congar, O.P., address this problem. He said that for the church to be relevant to contemporary Western man or woman two things were needed. First, he said, it must be a church *for* God, and by that he meant a church that makes available to all people the transcendent and contemplative dimensions of Christian tradition. His second point was that it must be a church for human liberation, seen as existing *for others*. Congar insisted that relevancy depended on both movements being honored even though that was admittedly difficult. He was pointing to wholeness.

Monastic openness to the laity, as discussed earlier in the chapter, is certainly one significant contribution to wholeness. Centers and institutes devoted to deepening contemplative awareness among active, busy people are also valuable resources. But both monasteries and institutes reach small numbers. Parishes and congregations, the hubs of ordinary spiritual journeying, are rich in possibilities for supporting genuine sabbath for their people. For example:

- Early morning meditation groups have been tried and incorporated into some parishes. One suburban parish held a weekly meeting of quiet prayer, based on *lectio divina*, from 6:30 to 7:15 in the morning, allowing workers time to board the train into the city. (*Lectio divina* is an ancient monastic method of meditative prayer based on spiritual reading of the Scriptures. One reads a short passage and when a word arrests the attention, the pray-er stops there and uses the word as the means of going deeper into the recesses of the soul. After a time of resting with the word, the pray-er responds to the Spirit with some form of active prayer.)

- One day a week the parish church might be kept open for quiet prayer. Even in these days of concern over theft and vandalism, the open church is possible *if* the priest, minister, or lay leader will devote a day to being in the church, a prayerful, hospitable presence, enabling others to come and simply be.

- It is important that someone on the parish staff — or some gifted member of the community — is willing to serve as a spiritual guide for those who are on an intentional spiritual pilgrimage and who are in need of soul friends. Training should be provided for those who are so called and gifted.

A parish committed to supporting sabbath rest in some form ultimately may do less, but what activity it does undertake will come from a sense of call. Both the Hebrew Scriptures and the principles of good agriculture teach us that after the land lies fallow a rich harvest will follow.

Not everyone has access to a Trappist monastery. The parish church may not be able to undertake the practices noted above. And clearly not everyone will be drawn to the cloister as a way of life. Nor should one look to an illness for a doorway into silence. There are ways, however, of structuring ordinary life to include this essential ingredient for spiritual growth and development. The first and most important step in structuring solitude and silence is desire. Do we believe in the importance of time apart and alone, and do we want to enter that doorway? When we can say we want solitude, the next step is to review the structure of a typical day or week to see the possibilities therein.

Practical Suggestions

Take a walk. City streets, bike paths, parks, and suburban neighborhoods have large numbers of runners, joggers, and walkers. I'm told by friends who jog or run that these activities do, indeed, promote some solitude in one's life. Walking is what I know best. I like my walk in early morning, just at or after sunrise. I've come to know the two-mile route quite well, and so I don't need to devote much attention to where I'm going. Over the years, the morning walk (or occasionally in late afternoon) has become a time to lay before Christ a whole raft of concerns. In the Rahner vein I sometimes lament my repeated failings with one thing or another. Often I'm discoursing about the people I love and worry about: a grandchild who is ill, another who is having school problems, anxiety over a son's employment situation. There are neighbors with life-threatening illnesses, and misunderstandings with a friend. All these are drawn out and named. As I go through my list I will acknowledge that in the order of magnitude these are not much. These are not natural disasters like tornadoes or human disasters like the genocide in Rwanda. And then these faraway places — and people — are in my mind and in my heart. All the time he is listening. And out of the listening, sometimes, there comes a prod, a word, a pointing. I return home more attuned to the world, wanting to be more faithful. The walk is an experience of solitude, certainly, but before it is over, others are with us. There is company on the spiritual pathways.

Some walkers seek simply to observe, and in so doing to sharpen attentiveness. Journalist Edward Fischer is of the opinion that one of the healthiest things you can do is to aspire to the high calling of a pedestrian. "I walk for results not measured by instruments. What a walk does for the spirit is more important than what it does for the cardiovascular system."[35] The uncluttered time and space which a solitude walk offers can be effective in deepening one's perception of the universal — Thich Nhat Hanh's ultimate dimension — that can be seen behind every particular: every bird, rose, winding pathway, flower arrangement, pile of leaves.

Connect with nature. Every season is an offering of nature to move us into the spirit of contemplation. Winter presents us with the barest outlines, the simplicity of empty branches against the cold skies. Snow carries us into the silence of the season as whiteness layers our world, transforming it without a sound.

Spring reminds us that life slumbers beyond the apparent bleakness of winter. Tight buds become blossoms and leaves; suddenly (or so it seems) the earth is awash in pastels, and a subtle hum can be heard, the hint of life beginning again. Summer turns the hum into a symphony: birds, ocean waves, children's laughter. Heat invites us into quietude.

Autumn announces the end of a cycle with a blast of color. Trees become bright daring banners while underfoot one hears the crunch of departed leaves. The late-day light changes. The moon seems cooler. Expectations are in the air.

Simply observing the signs of nature all around us can afford moments of solitude. Attention to nature's sounds, sights, touches — bird song, crunchy leaves, the smallest breeze, the feel of rain, the scent of honeysuckle, the surprising sculptures of winter ice — can become moments of solitude.

John O'Donohue speaks of the landscape concealing a vast presence. "The shape of a landscape is an ancient and silent form of consciousness," he writes. "The earth is full of soul."[36]

So use the landscape which frames your life as a way to solitude and silence.

Tend a garden. For many, gardening is a specific gateway to what O'Donohue calls the loyalty of earth's stillness. A young woman I know well who gardens in a large communal plot shared this about her experience.

> When I go to the garden alone I go to a different place in myself. Because of this I can be more alone in the garden than anywhere else, even when there are other gardeners working nearby. And the silence of the garden is large, even while the normal sounds of life can be heard.
>
> I can experience this solitude and silence while I work in the garden because my mind empties and clears and time ceases to exist. If there is any heaviness in my life, it is

lifted, it dissipates, and I am lighter. In creating order in the garden there is order in my life.

I work slowly without haste. I put seeds and seedlings in the ground. I water and weed and tend and wait. But the waiting isn't hard because it's the process of the garden that gives pleasure and peace. To be able to pick vegetables in the end is a gift. People often remark about what a good gardener I am to be able to grow this food and bring it to the table. And I never know what to say — all I do is tend the garden. God is the one who grows the vegetables.[37]

Notice the life cycle. Certain stages in the life cycle are natural settings for fostering solitude in one's life. The care of a baby, especially for mothers who nurse, often creates the space for contemplative stillness. Watching young children play, absorbed in the imaginative world they have created, also enables the mind and spirit to be still, to watch, to wait.

Old age — or growing older — is particularly blessed in terms of solitude and silence. The natural diminishments that come with aging carve out for us spaces in which to reflect on the great gift of life which has been and is ours. In truth, this stage of life can be richly creative. One can stand still in the present moment, resting in the revelations of nature and the silence of the *now,* as well as a remembrance of things past. O'Donohue believes that we will discover that stillness can be a great companion as it heals the fragmented parts of our lives.[38] Of course it takes courage to enter into the silence of old age, as it does for any stage of life. But the temptation, when one has more discretionary time than at any other stage in life, is to trivialize leisure and to "fill up one's life" with diversions rather than with attentiveness and purpose. The church and other religious/spiritual entities can help older people, indeed *all* people, to appreciate this last gift of time.

A final word. Solitude and silence are not the same as lone-
liness and alienation. "When you come into your solitude," says
O'Donohue, "you come into companionship with everyone and
everything."[39] I believe this expansive and inclusive companionship with all of life is mediated through a visible community,
which is the other side of solitude.

Third Essential

AUTHENTIC COMMUNITY

Behold, how good it is, and how pleasant,
where brethren dwell at one! . . .
For there the LORD has pronounced his blessing,
life forever.

(PSALM 133:1, 3)

T HE TRAPPISTS, formed in an environment of silence and solitude, will tell you that equally important in their spiritual
growth and development is their belonging to a community of
common cause. The monks help one another to be faithful to
their chosen way of life: rising at 3:30 in the morning for the first
common prayer of the day and undertaking the manual labor by
which they economically support their way of life, whether that
be cheese making or farming. Together they strengthen one another's vocation and remind each other of the call of God in
their lives.

Community is not peculiar to Christian monastic orders. Buddhists, too, know the importance of a community in which all the
members are sharing the same practice. "In fact," writes Thich
Nhat Hanh, "it is crucial to be with a Sangha[40] or a church where
everyone practices together, or dwells mindfully in the Spirit. We
need to create such communities for our own benefit."[41] He goes
on to say that the community need not be perfect. What counts
is that each member remain faithful to the practices and encourage one another along the way, opening up our separate selves

59

to form one body. Christians will recognize in the Buddhist vision of community components of the doctrine of the Body of Christ.

Serious spiritual pilgrims have always sensed that the other side of solitude is, indeed, community — a committed life with others. As one enters more deeply into the life of prayer there is the realization that we do not exist for ourselves, but for others: the opposite of the sharp individualism which characterizes much of modern Western life. In silence and solitude our attention is honed, enabling us to become more present — and attentive — to those with whom we work and live, and even beyond our immediate environment to the poor and needy who are not personally known to us.

Benedictine John Main and Thich Nhat Hanh are in substantial agreement that we find our true selves when we are wholly turned toward those with whom we live. In such a stance we are not seeking to manipulate another but to reverence him or her. Main writes that Christian community is in essence the experience of being held in reverence by others and we, in our turn, reverencing them.[42] This does not suppose a bland sameness or total unanimity in terms of ideas and principles. Differences are possible and can even spark a creative dynamic, if we hold one another, including our differences, in mutual respect.

The First Letter to the Corinthians

One of the most vivid portraits of the church fully alive is found in Paul's first letter to the church at Corinth. Paul speaks there of a community where the members exercise a variety of gifts for the benefit of the whole. He is careful to note that showier gifts, like speaking in unknown tongues or prophesying, are not to be considered superior. Everyone's giftedness is needed, he insists, in order for the community to thrive. He likens the community to the Body of Christ and eloquently exalts the humble parts of the body, an encouragement to all.

His emphasis on gifts is the clarion call to a creative life, aligned with the creativity of the Holy Spirit. "And now there are varieties of gifts, but the same Spirit; and there are varieties of services, but the same Lord; and there are varieties of working, but it is the same God who inspires them all in everyone. To each is given the manifestation of the Spirit for the common good" (1 Cor. 12:4–7).

There is an ecumenical church in Washington, D.C. (the Church of the Savior) which is organized according to the theology of gifts as found in 1 Corinthians. The pastor believes that the church today is still gifted by God for the good of all. He contends that one of the tasks of a rich and joyful life is to discover our particular gifts, and that the church has an important role to play in our discovery. The gifts, growing out of one's true self, are the outward expression of that self. To use them in the service of others is not only to help some segment of human need, but to experience one's true self. Peace and blessing flow from these authentic activities.

The second priority of this church, after the discovery and cultivation of gifts, is for the members to be actively engaged in outward mission, a compassionate and intelligent presence in a world full of pain and despair. The mission is undertaken by small groups — small communities — within the larger framework of the church. The small community is the site for personal and spiritual growth and for attentiveness to God's call to mission. There are mission groups dedicated to affordable housing, to hospital care for sick street people, to retreat work, to formation for public service, to group homes for troubled or abandoned children — and more. New mission groups are continually formed as God's Spirit directs the church to minister to the needs of the wider society, which may change according to the current cultural and political situation. Because people are asked to serve in accord with their own gifts and talents, intuitions and insights, the mission and the service are vehicles of personal renewal. If one feels called to try something different, the group discerns how that might work; and people are often stretched in new directions.

Informal Communities

Many parishes have in recent years set about inviting people to join small communities of shared faith and shared mission. While not formally constructed along the lines of the Church of the Savior these small communities, in various forms and designs, are an important means of spiritual growth. Over the years I have been blessed by belonging to several small communities. They have not been sponsored by a single parish, but have been comprised of members from different churches.

The earliest community was the mothers' prayer group mentioned in the first chapter. We were unused to meeting without a priest (who was typically called a chaplain decades ago), so our gathering each week (without a chaplain) was an adventure of sorts, although an adventure that required careful planning, for example, the care of our preschool children, a rotating responsibility. Leadership of the prayer group also rotated. We were all learning together. We wanted to experience extended silence, to enter with faith into intercessory prayer, to practice scriptural meditation, and to open ourselves to the Holy Spirit, alone and together. All this, and more, came to pass.

I had been reading Evelyn Underhill's works and shared with the group her urging that those who embark on a way of prayer give more time and attention to direct communion with God. We had been deeply touched by the power of our intercessory prayer for one another, as prayer after prayer opened the way to resolution of personal and family problems. But Under-hill pressed those who met as prayer groups to practice putting their whole lives at God's disposal. We trustingly entered into periods of extended silence, intentionally doing as Underhill sug-gested. Eventually some members felt drawn in new directions, one to counseling work, another to advanced education, and others to more regular ministry within their parishes. Their faith-fulness and trust enabled God's word to be carried into places of darkness and pain. Their work has matured with them. Many of us have remained friends even as our lives have unfolded in different ways.

There were other small communities through the years. One was organized around studying and praying the Scriptures. A priest was part of our regular meetings and we often con-cluded our meditation, prayer, and life-sharing with Eucharist. We gained the courage from one another to jointly help a man who had been in prison for many years, constructing a parole plan for him and trying to provide resources as he attempted a life outside the prison walls. Together we found the will to be his friend.

For about two decades now my husband and I have belonged to a small community devoted originally to study, prayer, and reflection. Several couples have remained from the beginning, providing some institutional memory. One of the original mem-bers, a widow, entered a Benedictine convent eighteen years ago, and we feel sustained by her prayers. A couple who joined us later in our common life divorced, a traumatic experience for everyone. There have been misunderstandings and hurts and suggestions that we dissolve. But something greater than our individual selves holds us together.

About ten years ago the community felt called to undertake a common action about a problem in our local community, namely, the dearth of affordable housing. Eight people with one thou-sand dollars set out to buy garden apartments that were up for sale and likely to be bought by big developers. Nudged by the Spirit we formed a coalition of local government, churches, the building industry, and individuals — a partnership, we called it — to preserve and improve affordable rental properties in our civic community. Today, the partnership owns several hundred units, has a staff, and is recognized as a consistent advocate for those at the bottom of the economic ladder.

At first, community members did everything on a volunteer basis. When we held our monthly community meeting, little time was given to personal or spiritual conversation. Housing was at the center. When we could catch our breath we realized that something had to change. We invited new members into the group, asked a woman skilled in spiritual direction to be our pastoral leader, and set out upon a course of further study. Now the housing project has a life of its own, and our small community continues its life, moment by moment, not knowing what changes are ahead. We are convinced, however, that God's Spirit guided us in what seemed the impossible task of establishing a new nonprofit agency. Our logo reads, "In the shelter of one another, the people live." That could also be said of our life together in this particular community.

A number of movements and associations have small communities at the center of their vision. *Equipes des Notre Dame* is one. The English translation is "Teams of Our Lady." The name can be misleading. A friend of long standing told me that when she and her husband were approached twenty years ago about joining the teams, her instinctual response was that she was not interested in an exclusively Marian movement. However, she and her husband did want a deeper spirituality, and that led them to consider the movement in a more open way. They learned that the Teams of Our Lady is not another organization or parish activity, but *a way of life*. It takes at least a year of study and serious reflection before a couple is ready to subscribe to the obligations — team members say opportunities — which are suggested as a way of growth in marriage. The emphasis, it must be noted, is on marriage — not family per se. The "opportunities" include daily prayer as a couple and as individuals; a monthly "sitting down" to discuss those areas of a couple's life that need to be reviewed or examined; development of a personal rule of life, including prayer and action; and a monthly meeting with five or six couples together with a chaplain, yet another form of small Christian community.

My friend says that while the "sit downs" are very important to the couple because then they can discuss the problem areas outside a climate of accusation and anger, so too are the monthly meetings with other team members. "During the monthly meeting and shared meal couples help one another by sharing how the month has been in terms of both personal experiences and obligations and offer suggestions which have proved useful. There is gentle understanding of the couple who says, 'We've had a bad month!' There is also affirmation of couples who have made progress in prayer and communication."

An important element in the communal life of teams is the annual retreat. The chaplain is certainly important to the retreat (and indeed the overall life of the team), but others — ordinary men and women who are husbands and wives and parents — share responsibility for the retreat presentations, providing an enriched opportunity for all. It is not unusual that team members become extended families to each other, supportive companions in times of loss and times of glorious joy.[43]

Some communities are more structured than the informal ones. They have a clear identity and are often associated with a specific place, much like the monasteries. Two communities formed since the Second World War, each with a well-defined spirituality, are the St. Egidio Community and the Brothers of Taizé.

St. Egidio

One of the loveliest piazzas in Rome is that of St. Egidio, named for the small church at its center. That church also gives its name to a relatively new community of lay men and women, and priests.

One perfect autumn evening a few years ago I visited the piazza, the church, and the community. I had come for the evening prayer which the community celebrates there every night. As I took my place I was handed headphones for simultaneous translation. The church, small and rather exquisite, quickly filled up with people of all ages and nationalities. A well-dressed man carrying a briefcase walked purposefully down the aisle and into the sanctuary. He sat down on one of the risers that serve as sanctuary seats. Women in blazers, young men in jeans and sweaters, business people and students — ordinary people — streamed into the sanctuary. This was the community at prayer, and we visitors were joining with them.

They sat meditatively, like monks rooted in their monastery. Someone rose to light candles on the simple altar. Then the music began. A capella chants filled the holy space and poured into the piazza. A young man who looked like a student preached. After the prayer, the community members quietly departed, as purposefully as they had entered. They were going home to spouses and dinners and preparation for tomorrow's work.

I sat a while, savoring the beauty and simplicity of the experience. Then Claudio, one of the original members of the community, invited me to a neighborhood trattoria where over pasta and wine I learned more details about the St. Egidio community.

Over thirty years ago a young man, then eighteen years old, sat in the run-down church (now beautifully restored), and asked the Holy Spirit for guidance concerning the direction of his life.

A few other young people joined him in his prayer. Together they waited on God. These few seekers were the beginning of what would grow into one of the most dynamic new communities of the twentieth century. They soon felt themselves drawn to evangelization and solidarity with the poor. As they continued in prayer their commitment grew, and so did their numbers.

The first act of compassionate service by the St. Egidio founders was directed to the needs of children, especially those most neglected. To their daily prayer they added regular visits to abandoned children who were housed in various Roman institutions.

Next they turned their attention to Gypsy children badly in need of schooling. The young people of St. Egidio used a creative approach to what many considered a hopeless task. Rather than trying to coax the children to come to a traditional schoolroom, they decided to teach them in abandoned buses near Gypsy encampments. Members of the community are still teaching these youngsters the rudiments of reading and communication in surroundings familiar to the children. The educational establishment might be horrified, but the St. Egidio method works for these children.

The community now numbers approximately fifteen thousand and can be found in many Italian cities in addition to Rome and in other countries of Europe. They are also in South and North America and in Africa. But the heart of the community remains in the tiny church on the Piazza of St. Egidio.

One becomes a member of the community simply by choosing to live the St. Egidio vocation, namely, faithful listening to the Gospel in prayer, both personal and liturgical; prompt service to the poor; and support and care for one another. There is no formal joining. The members are ordinary people living ordinary lives faithful to their families and to their various professions.

Peacemaking is another central concern of the community. The members were among the organizers of the day of Prayer for Peace, which Pope John Paul II convened in Assisi in October of 1986. This interreligious prayer event gave hope to people everywhere that understanding, reconciliation, and respect for differences are all possible even in troubled places with a history of hatred. Thirty years before no one believed that representatives of Islam, Buddhism, and Hinduism, and members of a Native American tribe would be at prayer with the pope. But there were men and women, prominent among them the St. Egidio community, who could imagine such an event and who were willing to work and work hard to give flesh to the vision. One of St. Egidio's continuing tasks is to organize the annual International Meeting of Prayer for Peace.

They do more than that. They act on their prayer. Through what has been called an active diplomacy of friendship, the community has been involved in peaceful negotiations in many war-ravaged countries. It helped to broker a long sought peace treaty in Mozambique, for example. The community has been nominated for the Nobel Peace Prize several times.

The St. Egidio Community has something to teach all serious spiritual seekers. The first is that God's call often begins with something very small: a mustard seed, or a teenager at prayer in a run-down church. We also see how the many gifts of members can be utilized and developed in service to a larger reality. Perhaps most importantly, St. Egidio demonstrates how relationships are the heart and soul of community life: relationship with God, with one another, with the poor, and with victims of war and injustice. There can be no genuine spiritual growth without attention to *all* of these relationships at some time, in some way.

Taizé

For years I had heard about the Taizé Community located in France near the ruins of the ancient Benedictine monastery of

Cluny. Like many, I loved the distinctive Taizé music and chants. I knew that the community consisted of Catholics and Protestants who lived a new kind of monastic life, some few of them ordained and all of them having taken vows as brothers in the community. But it was not until I journeyed to the tiny village in the Burgundy hills that I experienced first hand the spirit of Taizé.

Three times a day white-robed brothers from different nations and different religious denominations gather in the Church of Reconciliation for prayer. They are surrounded by young people who kneel or sit before the icons that grace the church, illuminated by candlelight. (At other times of the day the white robes give way to blue jeans.) Brother Roger, founder of the Taizé community, is accompanied by children of the village, one of whom serves as the cantor, as did his mother a generation ago. Brother Roger is wrapped in an aura of humility and peace.

One enters the Taizé church — or any church where the Taizé prayer is offered — in silence. Soon the piercing melodies of the Taizé music fill the sacred space. Scripture is read, followed by more silence so that the word of God can sink into the deepest recesses of the heart. If Taizé is about anything it is about the mingling of the human heart with the heart of God.

At evening prayer the deepest kind of listening is encouraged. Toward the end of the prayer time priests rise from the gathered worshipers, recognizable by their stoles (a sacred vestment), used in the sacrament of reconciliation. The priests come to Taizé for their own spiritual enrichment, but in the evenings they are there to hear the confessions of the Catholics, mostly young people, who have been praying and studying during the course of the day. In large numbers the young people approach the waiting, listening priests. At the same time, some Taizé brothers are seen standing at the edge of the congregation, available to those who are not of the Catholic community but who wish to share something of the heart, a burden perhaps, or a newly kindled desire for God. Taizé offers young and old an unencumbered language to speak about things that are often too deep for words.

Noticeable in the community is a sense of authentic respect for differences, whether they be differences of race, religion, or national origin. It has been said that we live in a world of permeable borders. With increasing ease we pass into the spheres of different others, those whose cultural experiences and languages are different, who pray differently, and who may image God very differently. The Taizé experience says look beyond the differences to our common search for meaning.

Both communities, St. Egidio and Taizé, model some of the essential characteristics of authentic community as differentiated from groups based on isolation and alienation. For one thing, they are both centered around the age-old tradition of monastic prayer, updated it is true, but readily recognizable as being in the ancient lineage. For another they both put their prayer into action, serving the poor in concrete ways.

The brothers of Taizé organize a type of retreat called the Pilgrimage of Trust on Earth, and they take the pilgrimage to those cities in the world badly in need of reconciliation and trust. They welcome young people of all religions and no religion, themselves trusting that God will guide their work. The brothers' prayer is one I frequently voice, "O God, give me energy to do your work," applicable to the routines of family life, the discipline of writing, or the monotony of a particular church ministry. I find the prayer braces me when I feel like quitting.

Both St. Egidio and Taizé are deeply committed to works of peace, to nonviolence, to building a society of justice and compassion. Neither community actively seeks members, but like the scriptural description of light on the lampstand, they emit a glow which others see and to which they are drawn.

Authentic community is found in many places. Buddhists believe that a true community, a Sangha, can be transforming if the Six Concords (agreements) are practiced. The concords are sharing space, sharing essentials of daily life, observing the same precepts, using only words that contribute to harmony, sharing our insights and understanding, and respecting each other's viewpoints.[44]

While informal communities, a prayer group, or a mission community may not practice fully the Six Concords (for example, it is unusual for a prayer group to intimately share space) many of the concords do apply. And they are amazingly applicable to families who are trying to live a centered life. You can readily see a subtext in the concords, a call to truthfulness and honesty, self-control and humility. They are remarkably aligned with the description of love found in the first Letter to the Corinthians. "Love is patient, love is kind. It is not jealous, is not pompous, it is not inflated. It is not rude, it does not seek its own interests, it is not quick tempered. It does not brood over injury. It does not rejoice over wrongdoing but rejoices with the truth. It bears all things, believes all things, hopes all things, endures all things. Love never fails" (1 Cor. 13:4–8).

Community and Society

Small communities need larger realities like the church so that the memory of ultimate purpose not be lost. The wisdom of Scripture and tradition, for example, reminds Christians that St. John the Evangelist teaches that we lie if we maintain that we love God while hating our neighbor. John Main drives home the point in equally direct fashion. He says we must be clear about what St. John is saying, which is "we cannot love God *or* our neighbor. We love both or neither."[45]

Authentic communities imbued with the divine light will certainly have an impact on the social order. One dramatic example is illustrated in the documentary film *Weapons of the Spirit,* the work of Pierre Sauvauge. It is the story of a small village in the French mountains, Le Chambon sur Lignon, during the period of Nazi occupation of France during World War II. The people of Le Chambon are descendents of Protestant Huguenots, and a strong biblical, evangelical tradition has flourished there over the centuries.

The filmmaker, who is Jewish, was born in Le Chambon in the early 1940s. Through the years he had heard from his parents how remarkable the people of that region were. Each and every villager and farm family in the region harbored Jewish refugees during the War. No one was refused. As a result five thousand children were saved from death camps, along with countless adults, all because the people of Le Chambon acted upon their spiritual convictions.

The pastors of the Protestant church opened a school where village children and the Jewish refugees were educated side-by-side. Farmers stretched their food to feed their many unexpected guests. One young villager worked night and day to forge identity papers through the French underground, enabling passage into Switzerland. No one was ever turned away.

Some of the villagers were still alive when Sauvauge was making his film. They are luminous on the screen, having aged with beauty and grace. When asked why they endangered their lives to harbor strangers, their eyes reveal the depth of their compassion. Their replies are simple and forthright. "We could not turn them away," they said. "They came from God. It was like the Old Testament alive in our midst."

The people of Le Chambon saw nothing unusual in their saving actions. Over and over they commented, "We never thought about it." And the Nazis never interfered, either through ignorance or indifference.

One sees in *Weapons of the Spirit* the fruit of genuine spiritual formation: an entire community, civic as well as religious, caught up in life-giving, transforming power. There was nothing throughout France to equal the weapons of the spirit employed on behalf of righteousness in Le Chambon. One senses that the villagers not only readily saw the sacred in the extraordinary ("They [the Jewish refugees] came from God"), but the villagers had been prepared for their courageous actions by noticing the holy presence in the most ordinary routines of daily life: food, shelter, books, prayer.

Practical Suggestions

Monasteries, Sanghas, and communities like St. Egidio and Taizé may be beyond our immediate reach, but they invite us to experiment with the formation of contemporary community. You may not be able to travel to Rome or to Burgundy, but there are other ways to tap into their priorities.

Look for Taizé prayer. A number of churches, Catholic and Protestant, have regular prayer services modeled on Taizé. The National Cathedral of Sts. Peter and Paul, for example, in Washington, D.C., conducts Taizé Evening Prayer on Sunday evenings. Several churches in Dayton, Ohio, also conduct Taizé services. The religion section of local newspapers often carry this information.

Ask your pastor. Ask your pastoral leaders to help facilitate the formation of a small community. There are many resources, biblical and pastoral, for beginning communities.

Invite some friends. Invite those who share with you the same desire or hunger to follow a spiritual way to meet and explore the possibilities for forming a small community. Together you will gain both insight and strength; you will encourage and embolden one another.

Seek out movements within the wider church which foster small groups like Teams of Our Lady. Your church headquarters can help you in your search.

Fourth Essential

DISCOVERING THE SACRED IN THE ORDINARY

*As the rising sun is clear to all,
so the glory of the LORD fills all his works.*
(SIRACH 42:16)

ALFRED LORD TENNYSON plucked a flower from a crannied wall and after studying it, with full attention, wrote that *if* he could understand the flower, "root and all," he would know what God is and what the human person is. His short poem "Flower in a Crannied Wall" depicts the movement from particular, concrete experience to apprehension of universal truth.

"*If* I could understand." How does it happen, then, this understanding that deepens one's vision to such an extent that the sacred is visible in the ordinary stuff of life? In flowers and stone walls, for example?

Theologians, artists, and mystics all agree that attentiveness is a fundamental necessity. Be attentive, says Jesuit theologian Bernard Lonergan, if you want to move toward insight. And he means *be attentive* to your experience. Notice what is going on in your field of perception and your reservoir of feelings. You will recognize there outlines of Evelyn Underhill's portrayal of practical mysticism. Concentrate, really concentrate, on piano scales, or a geometric theorem, or a display of nature — and the Maker of all that wonder may be glimpsed.

75

Ordinary Sacramentals

In Nature. No one has been more attentive to the life all around him than the late naturalist Loren Eiseley. In clear and simple language characterized by imaginative observation, Dr. Eiseley leads one into the land of flowers and seeds, bugs and birds, earth and rivers. And he does so in the ordinary environments in which most of us live.

Every autumn he would set out on what he called the search for the secret of life. Dressed in his worn hat and an old jacket, he would make his way carefully down his apartment steps. Climbing over a nearby wall he'd venture into an unkempt field. Before long all kinds of seeds — the leavings of summer — were attached to him.

He especially liked the fall season for the examination of life's secrets. The seeds, clinging to him, always held much promise. In summer there is too much activity, too much lushness and humming, he believed.

> As I grow older and conserve my efforts, I shall give this season [fall] my final and undivided attention. I shall be found standing bemused in a brown sea of rusty stems. Somewhere ... may lie the key to the secret. I shall not let it escape through lack of diligence or through the smiles of people in high windows. I am sure now that life is not what it is purported to be and that nature, in the canny words of a Scotch theologue, "is not as natural as it looks." I have learned this in a small suburban field.[46]

Others, too, alert us to life beyond the obvious. Poet Mary Oliver for one. The ordinary contents of her environment are transformed into lyrics of truth and beauty. Mushrooms, lightning, egrets, the first snow, roses, blackberries, bluefish, swamps — everything is numinous to her eye. She is respectful of the essence of life in its many forms.

I never thought at all about moles until I read her poem about them, how they are simply true to their natures:

> pushing and shoving
> with their stubborn muzzles against
> the whole earth,
> finding it
> delicious.[47]

Eiseley and Oliver, like Tennyson before them, discover the concrete reality of the sacred in the ordinary environment and share those discoveries in fresh and compelling language, blessing us in a way that religious abstractions rarely do. When I read a Mary Oliver poem I feel the lavishness of God. A few lines from Eiseley and I can appreciate anew the sacredness and power of life in ways seldom accessible to me in theological writing.

But still...I dwell in an apartment high above the Potomac River. An occasional song bird, lost perhaps, drops down to my small roof terrace, on his way to somewhere else. Nature is a bit remote at such heights. My daily contacts (except for morning walks and short forays to the seashore) are with books and kitchen utensils, desks and computers. Where is the divine mystery in the world of things?

In Things. I turn to Chilean poet Pablo Neruda, who was awarded the Nobel Prize for Literature. Among his many books are several volumes of odes to ordinary objects and everyday experiences. His "Ode to Things" pulsates with a passion for human creations which, he says, have become part of his being. There are many more odes, individual songs of praise to specific concrete objects; they rivet my attention. Spoons, for example. I handle spoons every day, but I never thought about their development or their daily companionship in the lives of people all over the world until I read "Ode to the Spoon." The act of setting the table assumes an enlarged meaning when I read of his hopes for a world without hunger where:

> . . . a total mobilization of spoons,
> will shed light where once was darkness
> shining on plates spread all over the table
> like contented flowers.[48]

Under Neruda's gaze the cat ("born in a state of total completion") and the dictionary ("ancient and weighty in its worn leather coat") are full of the rhythms of a life unnoticed until the poet's eye penetrated their unique reality.

Is it possible then for us, ordinary people, to study deeply the hidden life of the objects that fill our environments? The paintings, the photographs, the pots and pans, the inherited furniture, the wedding ring? I think so. And finding them praiseworthy is one step in the cultivation of a grateful heart and a centered soul.

Kathleen Norris has taken the daily routines of household work as the theme for her Madaleva lecture, published under the title of *The Quotidian Mysteries*. She begins with a quote from Gregory of Nyssa's *On the Lord's Prayer:*

> Let us remember that the life in which we ought to be interested is "daily" life. We can, each of us, only call the present time our own. . . . Our Lord tells us to pray for today, and so he prevents us from tormenting ourselves about tomorrow. It is as if [God] were to say to us: "[It is I] who gives you this day [and] will also give you what you need for this day, who makes the sun to rise, who scatters the darkness of night and reveals to you the rays of the sun."

Gregory of Nyssa, Kathleen Norris, Pablo Neruda, and a host of other thinkers and writers invite us to be attentive to the present moment, to the small tasks at hand that make up the measure of our days.

In Hymns and Canticles. I am writing these pages in a house by a small lake, a short walk to the ocean. It is early June, before summer vacationers arrive to fill the sand and surf and board-walk — and these lakeside houses — with their relaxing laughter. The church's morning prayer for this second week in Ordinary Time begins with the hymn of St. Patrick which invokes the familiar contents of life: "This day God sends me strength of high heaven." And what is that strength? It is "sun and moon shining, the flame in the hearth, the flash of lightning, the wind, the deepness of ocean, the firmness of earth." The basic elements in our world, available to all.

The canticle for this day, too, is a song of praise from one who has been delivered from the edge of death. The poignant pleasure in simply being alive gives rise to outbursts of joy. "The living, the living gives you thanks" cries Isaiah. And then, unable to contain himself, he declares, "We shall sing to stringed instruments."

I have felt like that. On those occasions when illness wanes, or a family member finds a good job (one that can provide not only a living but a life), or a friend comes back from the depths of depression — then I want to sing, to read poetry aloud, to let tears come as they will. Ordinary acts like preparing a meal, holding a child, sitting with one's beloved are suffused with gratitude and grace. It is the near loss, or recovery, of some small piece of our ordinary life — not the grand gestures — that cleanses our vision so we can see the grandeur of God always present.

Everyday Blessings

Over the years I have received letters from people in different parts of the country and in different life circumstances whose stories are really testimonies from ordinary life, accounts of people living the beatitudes, aware of being blessed. The circumstances of their lives, their reflection on these circumstances, their prayer and willingness to align themselves with God have enabled them, unself-consciously, to be the salt of their particular corner of the earth and light for their fellow humans. Analyzing these testimonies one discovers that the family, the workplace, and the civic arena are where blessedness is most evident. They see the contours of the sacred in the web of their relationships, in the work of their hands, and in their various public responsibilities.

In the Family.

- A wife tends her wheelchair-bound husband, and over time has come to see Christ in her husband's responses to her, and in his efforts (often frustrating) to care for himself.

- Parents watch the almost miraculous development of their infant into a child with intelligence and will, and they are in awe.

- An abused wife, alone in bed before sunrise, decides that this day she will remove herself and her daughter from the abusive environment, and she knows with all her being that her courage has come from God.

- Teenagers write about their small sisters and brothers who in their spontaneity and joy relieve adolescent anxiety. "My little sister makes me laugh, and I forget about what's been bothering me," says one teen.

Birthdays and anniversaries, graduations and weddings — and funerals — highlight for us the splendor in the ordinary. The special occasions hold up for us the tapestry that the everyday routines are weaving. And we see how common threads, in God's hands, become a thing of uncommon beauty.

In the Workplace.
People testify to the links between home and work. There was a time when sociologists were convinced

that family and the workplace were two absolutely separate realities, with little influence upon one another. Current sociology as well as management theory now recognize the error in that position. It is *one* person, the same person, who lives in a family, goes to work, lives in a neighborhood, belongs to a church, and is a citizen of the nation and of the world. While it is true that many people present a different face in each of these settings, a person intentionally living out of a spiritual center will consciously try to forge the connections, to integrate the different strands of life, and to present the *one* face, the true face to the world. Their testimonies are inspiring. One correspondent from the West Coast wrote that habits established in the home become habits practiced elsewhere; the caring and consideration we give family members on a daily basis overflow to those we work with and for.

- A community health nurse with over twenty-five years experience wrote of the challenge she faced from supervisors who hadn't learned the difference between power and authority and who too often ranked finances above the needs of people. She had to call on God to help her speak her own truth. She also said that she learned a great deal about herself from a co-worker whom she found difficult, finally realizing that the co-worker mirrored many of her own shortcomings.

- A retired woman who was an information operator for the telephone company during World War II and who also worked as a waitress from time to time wrote, "These were person-to-person jobs, intimate and of service. As I worked I would say a prayer as I handed a glass of water to a customer."

- A ballet teacher spoke of the destructiveness of emphasizing competition over all else. She said that technical improvement is only a by-product of the spiritual encounter that true teaching really is.

- A junior high school teacher echoed the ballet instructor, saying that he tries to bring out the best in each student, and the best will be different for each.

- A clinical lab technician in Maine, working in the field of infertility, experiences her work as a "call" which she accepted only after much prayer and soul searching. She sees her work as promoting life and supporting the hopes of infertile couples. "All our clients are treated with respect and with a sense of sacredness," she says.

- The wife of a painter and paper hanger wrote me about a conversation she and her husband had one night about his work. He said that house painting sometimes poses ethical challenges for him. In the heat of competition and cutting costs the company tries to save in ways that bother the painter, doing one coat when the contract calls for two. He also noted the rather widespread abuse of going home early. But there is also delight in his work. "I like to think I bring beauty to the world in the hanging of beautiful wallpaper; even plain wallpaper or vinyl brings a look of cleanliness and orderliness."

- Sometimes careful attentiveness to the details of one's life will lead to unexpected work, to work that furthers the compassion of God. A physician, discovering the depths of his sympathy for patients recently widowed and concerned about their grieving process, shared his concern with some other physician friends. This conversation led to the establishment of a support group for those who grieve, an initiative of the several physicians who were convinced of the need.

- Similarly, a disabled woman, now bed-bound, wrote the following. "I have not been formally employed for twelve years. Having been an active wife, mother, and career woman, it took me only four years to find something I could do with my life that would be meaningful to me and hopefully pleasing to God. In order to maintain my sanity while lying in bed day after day, I began recording all my thoughts, feelings, and emotions. This process, in time, led me to believe that possibly I had a word that could be used to help others. A column for the Multiple Sclerosis Association resulted, and that column developed into another for the local newspaper. I added a new venture to my columns, a newsletter which I began for the community of newly built homes. The objective of the newsletter was to engender harmony and cooperation among neighbors and ultimately to build a community of common cause." She concluded her letter with these words. "In retrospect I suppose this writing can now be considered my work, though I never thought of it that way until I put these thoughts on paper for you."[49]

What do we see in these first-hand accounts of encountering the sacred in the ordinary dailiness of one's life? *First* is the importance of reflection on experience, as encapsulated in the last story above. Reflection is often stimulated by a simple question, such as the one I posed in my article. (One letter I received was from an eighty-eight-year-old blind woman who read the article in braille and who said she had been waiting a lifetime for someone to ask her what she knew about God.) Spiritual guides, small faith communities, spiritual movements, parishes — all, at some time and with frequency, must ask one another, "What do you now know about Christ? About the Spirit? About the fullness of God?"

Second, one sees a form of oscillation between being focused on the interior life (what is happening within) and acting on the insights available. The oscillation does not favor one movement over the other; rather, those who have a keen awareness of the sacred in the ordinary are attentive to both movements, being neither quietist nor activist. They hold the two in tension, pulling them toward the center.

Third, there are certain dynamic qualities in their lives no matter what the particularities of their family or work. For example:

- Duty is a lifeline for them, not a deadening burden. And clearly the Spirit enlivens their duty.

- They recognize the deep power in forgiveness, and they tirelessly are willing to begin again. (Sometimes, however, beginning again means beginning anew, as in the case of the abused wife who left her husband.)

- Gratitude grows larger within them as they grow older. Life is recognized as the precious gift it is, and has always been.

- Good work is valued as a means of spiritual formation in it-self. Thomas Merton once wrote that a Shaker chair looked like it was made by someone who believed an angel might sit on it. And so, too, a well-tilled field, an imaginative lesson plan, a delicious meal, a carefully crafted piece of prose — all these are filled with the effort and skill and discipline of the worker, the person, who bears the image of God. And perhaps angels are close by.

Aligned with God, Creating from Life

All the contents of one's life, the sufferings as well as the pleasures, are raw material for creativity. The life and work of Clyde Connell illustrate this point. Mrs. Connell, who died in 1998 at the age of ninety-seven, became a full-time artist in her sixties.

Except for some traveling (to New York City, for instance) she spent her entire life in the Shreveport area. A lengthy obituary in the *New York Times* described how she used brown earth and red clay — the stuff of her homeland — to color her drawings and sculptures, which were often made from bits of iron scrap that her son found in his cotton fields. Her husband was a superintendent of a penal farm and some of her first serious paintings were made of black prisoners in the 1950s.

In 1952 she traveled to New York City to do social work with the Presbyterian Church; in New York she encountered the world of abstract expressionist paintings, and she returned often to the Museum of Modern Art to view these works. By the early 1960s she had a studio in Louisiana and was working full time as an artist, keeping up with developments in contemporary art through reading and traveling. In that period she began making assemblages of wood and iron held together by a mixture of paper and glue. She used this mixture as a building material which she colored with dirt, reinforced with sticks, and embedded with found metal. The results, according to the obituary writer, were powerful objects that suggested decorated trees and towers and costumed shamans. She had a mystical view of nature and described her drawings as transcriptions of its music, which she mysteriously heard on the bayou. Her work can be found in a number of museums, including the Metropolitan Museum of Art.[50]

I give this rather lengthy account of Mrs. Connell's creative life to point out that her early impetus to art arose from the difficulties which black prisoners had to live through on the penal farm. Her empathy drew her into closer examination of the realities before her. Later, she turned to the very ordinary elements that surrounded her life — dirt, scrap iron, sticks — to give expression to the essence of her world and give birth to a unique art form. What gift did she possess that allowed her to see a decorated tree in the scraps of wood and iron in her fields and in the red clay of her homeland?

Perhaps she had arrived at her true self. A friend, a Dominican friar, writes that we arrive at our true selves not so much through practice as through attitude:

> It is not a matter of whether we meditate or weed the garden, retire to a hermitage or go to the local bar. It is a matter of how and why we do these things; it is a question of attitude. What is this attitude? It is ... detachment. This immovable detachment brings about in us the greatest similarity with God, and as far as a creature can possess similarity to God, it must be by means of detachment.[51]

Consider the horizon of your life right now: the people, your work, the natural world, the inanimate world, your emotional world, your yearnings, your duties, your sorrows, the world's sorrows. Can you see these with the eye of God? Can you see the grace?

Practical Suggestions

One way to get in touch with the continual experience of the sacred in the ordinary is to keep a journal. The richness of one's own life experience can slip by, like water through our fingers, if we have no way to pause and observe our own expanding consciousness. So, in your journal:

Study your environment. In a detached way consider the concrete elements that are part of your life space. Look at your furniture, photographs, cooking utensils, works of art. Why do you have them? How do they affect your life? Do they speak to you of love, mercy, understanding?

Compose a poem. Or write several. Try writing from the point of view of some stable piece of your life: your cat, the garden, your grandmother's tablecloth, your front window. You may want to try writing an ode to some artifact, or person, or pet, or memory that is rooted in your life-space.

Write about your work. Try answering the question I posed to my readers some years ago, namely, how do you find the sacred dimension in your work, whether that be outside the home or within? You may want to use the fruits of the Spirit as found in Gal. 5:22–23 (love, joy, peace, patience, kindness, generosity, faithfulness, and self-control) as a touchstone for how the Spirit is present in the work of your hands (and your mind and imagination).

Reflect regularly. Weekly, or even daily, spend a few minutes reviewing those places, things, persons, situations, elements of nature where you glimpsed the sacred in the ordinary.

Fifth Essential

SAVORING

You anoint my head with oil, my cup overflows.

(PSALM 23)

ACCORDING TO THE *Random House Unabridged Dictionary,*
one definition of the verb "to savor" is to give oneself to
the enjoyment of — and the dictionary leaves us to fill in the
blank. Synonyms include "to relish," "to delight in," and "to appreciate." "Savoring" is not a term one frequently encounters in
reference to the spiritual life; yet it is a very important element.

St. Ignatius, in his introductory comments to *The Spiritual Exercises,* says that it is not *knowing much* that satisfies the soul, but
rather grasping things intimately and *savoring* them. This is particularly relevant to the person who during an Ignatian retreat
is reflectively moving through the salvation story. When something captures the attention, says the saint, it is best to linger
on the point, the word, the feeling, or the insight. The Spanish reads *sentir y gustar,* which one Jesuit scholar renders "to feel,
in an interior way, with the whole self." Because Christian spirituality is incarnational, the interior savoring will have external
dimensions. It is the whole person, after all, who savors.

A Dominican Friar

Jim is seventy-eight years old, a Dominican friar, ordained when
he was forty-two. During the past year he drove to Vermont

from North Carolina — a goodly distance — to preside at our daughter's wedding. For the last nine years he's walked with a cane, the result of having been run over by a bus on the border of Honduras and Guatemala. Nonetheless, he joyfully and enthusiastically agreed to celebrate the marriage.

His presence among us is memorable. I watch as he painstakingly makes his way to the second floor apartment our family has rented for the nuptial weekend. The bride's prewedding tea is just ending, and Jim and I organize the leftovers for a late lunch. He asks for a glass of red wine and then approaches the stale cucumber sandwiches with relish. We have been friends for a quarter of a century, and I notice how centered and peaceful he has become, how connected to the smallest things around him: the food, the wine, the clouds visible through the window. Later in the afternoon he explores the outdoors (while my husband and I rest) and brings us wild roses and an exuberant account of Vermont sunshine. He arranges the roses and gazes lovingly at them. Since his arrival, a few hours earlier, he has been *savoring* the bits and pieces of our Vermont world. His pure happiness makes me think of holiness, and of God's word: "I would feed with finest wheat and fill them with honey from the rock" (Psalm 81). Jim is now enjoying God's honey, after a lifetime of interior hunger and no little suffering.

A graduate of Harvard University, Jim served in the Second World War with the U.S. Air Corps. Memories of his role in the bombing missions over Japan haunted him for many years. When he spoke of the experience to fellow Dominican Shigeto Oshida, a former Zen Buddhist, Oshida simply laughed and said, "I was trying to shoot *you* down. Too bad I missed!" Oshida's realism lightened that particular burden for Jim, but others appeared, like the ogres that Jessica Powers wrote about in her poem "Old Bridge." There she describes how, as a child, she believed that ogres lived under a bridge she had to cross each day. When she grew up the fear changed:

Fled is that childish fear; my thoughts are couched
in grown-up wisdom now, and yet I find
that worse than ogres are the dark shapes crouched
lurking beneath the bridges of my mind.[52]

After the War, Jim worked for an oil company in China and
Hong Kong. That was followed by studies in Philosophy and Letters at the Universidad de México and a stint in the investment
banking business in Brazil. It was there that he reached the conclusion that he was being called to follow a different path in life.
He would often drop by a Benedictine monastery where the careful liturgy and solitude of the garden quieted him, for the moment.

One day a monk suggested that since Jim seemed to like the
monastic environment so much he should establish a perma-
nent residence in one, somewhere. That "somewhere" initially
was the Trappist Abbey at Gethsemani, where Thomas Merton
was student master.

Much about Trappist life was appealing: the silence, certainly,
and the presence of Thomas Merton, whose writings were an influence on him, as on many Catholics of that period. Strangely
enough Merton and he never exchanged words during Jim's year
at Gethsemani; monks did not converse in those days. During
that time he began some serious reading in theology, especially
Augustine and Aquinas, and slowly the thought grew in him that
his vocation might be different from plowing the fields (the manual labor assigned to him). He contacted the Dominicans with
whom he believed he could be more in touch with the church's
broad intellectual tradition, including teaching.

Theology was not the only pull toward the Dominicans. The
original idea of the founder, St. Dominic, was also attractive. The
image of an itinerant preacher, as Dominic was, in direct contact
with the poor was a powerful draw. It also mirrored, in a way, Jim's
own inner restlessness, which seemed harder and harder to satisfy.

His first assignment as a Dominican friar was teaching theology and philosophy to undergraduates. While teaching was intellectually and pastorally challenging, he wanted to continue his own studies in some systematic way. He thought Union Theological Seminary in New York City would be a good choice, and living in Harlem appealed to him. For several years he sought God in the city that never sleeps.

The search continued in Washington, D.C., and later in the country settings of southern Virginia and West Virginia. Finally he joined some other Dominicans who were on mission in Nigeria. All the while his health was deteriorating. There was back surgery, and then a serious bout of clinical depression. The latter led to hospitalization and near despair, as the dark shapes emerged from under the bridges of his mind.

Prayer, including the sacrament of the sick, and the perseverance of his religious community, which tirelessly searched for and finally found correct medical care, led him to a number of creative ministries: as Catholic chaplain at a major eastern university, as a hospital chaplain in a southern city, and as a priest-chaplain in a small mission in Central America, where he was when the bus he was running to catch caught his leg instead, crushing it. The bus driver got out of the bus, looked at Jim, got back on the bus and drove off. Some onlookers were more sympathetic. A pick-up truck was located and after a frantic five-hour trip he arrived in Guatemala City, where doctors wanted to amputate the damaged leg. The Dominicans wouldn't hear of it. Instead they sent him to Miami for leg reconstruction, and for a year of grueling physical therapy, painful and uncertain, but absolutely necessary if he were to walk again.

In the years following the accident he intensified his study of Zen meditation, always a part of his spiritual life, but now in the forefront of his personal horizon. Extended periods of time in two Zen monasteries confirmed this aspect of his vocation.

Pain awakens him often during the night, he told me, and when it does, instead of fighting the wakefulness, he *breathes*.

He watches his breath, he welcomes the Spirit. Awake or asleep, alive or dead, he is breathing his way through this wondrous pilgrimage of life, an embodiment of Psalm 150: "Let everything that lives and breathes, give praise to the Lord." And along the way Jim is savoring all that God spreads before him, sharing with others what he has been learning about pain and peace. In summer with migrant farm workers; in winter with men and women he meets in workshops and retreats.

Mindfulness: The Heart of Savoring

Jim has learned well the lessons of mindfulness, of being totally present to the moment. I often think of him as I glance at a small poster about eating mindfully. The poster is on a kitchen cupboard. The sayings are from a small book, *Present Moment, Wonderful Moment* by Thich Nhat Hanh, one of Jim's own mentors. They lead me through the steps of preparing and enjoying a meal. There is the empty plate to contemplate, soon to be filled with precious food. The food itself is fit for contemplation. I read,

> This plate of food
> so fragrant and appetizing
> also contains much suffering.

(Another friend likes to remind herself of all that has died that she might be nourished and live.)

The verses for beginning the meal read like a prayer:

With the first taste I promise to offer joy.
With the second I promise to help relieve the suffering of
    others.
With the third I promise to see others' joy as my own.
With the fourth I promise to learn the way of non-
    attachment and equanimity.

We are asked to be mindful of all the actions at the end of the meal, as well. With hunger satisfied one vows to live for the benefit of all being. Drinking tea centers the mind and the body. Even washing the dishes, if done with attention and love, will reveal a sacred dimension.

All kinds of ordinary people are practicing mindfulness, savoring the present moment. Catherine Walsh, former columnist for *America,* the Jesuit magazine, writing about a friend dying of a brain tumor, underscores the preciousness of a "normal day." The friend, a single mother of two, loved a poem called "Normal Day" by Mary Jean Irion. Walsh, meditating on the poem and on her friend's death, sees what a miracle it was and would be for her friend to once again have a normal day: to cook a family meal, or to share a Chinese meal, or to attend an art show opening.[53] Simple duties, simple pleasures.

The miracle of mindfulness in the savoring of ordinary life is a lens onto the sacred. To see through the lens, clearly, to savor the gift of the moment, requires a different experience of time.

Learning to Savor

Is age or injury the way into a different perception of time? At first it appears so. As Jim acquires years and faces crises his focus seems ever clearer and sharper. In some ways he is not unlike Lady Slane, the main character in Vita Sackville-West's novel *All Passion Spent.* In her mid-eighties, recently widowed, Lady Slane abandons the family home (much to the dismay of her sons and daughters) and retires to a small house in an English village. There she mulls over the decades of her rich life, but a life lived according to the expectations of others. Her own hopes of being a painter were never taken seriously in an age when families expected their daughters to marry, and marry well. But in the village, away from the social demands of London society, there is time to think about "the I" who loved Henry (her husband) and who shaped a life that suited him and others.

> She had plenty of leisure now, day in, day out, to survey her Life as a tract of country traversed, and at last become a landscape instead of separate fields or separate years and days, so that it became a unity and she could see the whole view, and could even pick out a particular field and wander around it again in spirit, though seeing it all the while as it were from a height, fallen into its proper place.[54]

She was, in fact, considering the lilies of the field, those in the meadows and those in the fields of her life. The savoring and integration were not only for her own final peace, however. Her great grand-daughter seeks her out, looking for strength and support as she, a younger version of Lady Slane, seeks a life of meaning.

It may be that with maturity comes a readiness for discerning what is important and for savoring it in praise of God. But the young, too, have the capacity to do so. In this matter we have the guidance of Jesus himself, who insists that unless we become as little children we cannot enter the Kingdom. What can he possibly mean? A common interpretation focuses on trust, namely, that as children trust their parents so we must trust God. And that is true, but incomplete. Observe children at play, especially in their preschool years. They play with an intense seriousness, concentrated as if *in* their play. Their focus is not diluted by many things. Even if a sand castle is destroyed by an ocean wave, the child (after understandable tears) is ready to start again.[55] This is one example of Søren Kierkegaard's insight that purity of heart is to will one thing. (And the pure of heart see God, we are told in Matthew 5.)

What happens to us between childhood and adulthood that diminishes our sense of wonder and the savoring of God's world, and of God? Each one will likely answer the question a bit differently; here, a spiritual guide can be of great assistance, helping to identify the various walls that have been constructed along the inner landscape. And sometimes a crisis serves as a kind of divine intervention to help us clear the field of rubble and concentrate on the treasure in the field (Matt. 13:44). So it was for Jim, I believe. The darkness of depression and later the agonizing re-building of his leg along with the accident's legacy of pain moved him to simplify desire, surely a factor in his ability to savor and celebrate life. It was not until Lady Slane was widowed that she could see her way clear to pursue her heart's desire.

One of the most gripping accounts of change rendered by way of tragedy is the story of writer Reynolds Price's life-threatening cancer. In 1984 a large cancer was discovered in his spinal chord; surgery failed to remove the growth. Price's very personal mem-oir, *A Whole New Life*, describes his journey from the time of discovery of the growth through radiation and medical treatment along with the spiritual experiences that swept into his life at that time. A novelist, poet, playwright, and Milton scholar, Price be-lieves the years since his catastrophic illness have been the most productive. Although he is confined to a wheelchair, it is as if some creative current has been set free. He says of his new life the following:

> I know this [new life] is better for me, and for most of my friends and students as well. . . . Paraplegia with its mad-dening limitations has forced a degree of patience and consequent watchfulness on me, though as a writer I'd al-ways been watchful. . . . Forced to sit, denied the easy flight that legs provide, you either learn patience or you cut your throat. . . . As I survived the black frustration of so many new forms of powerlessness, I partly learned to sit and at-tend, to watch and taste whatever or whomever seemed likely or needy, far more closely than I had in five decades. The pool of human evidence that lies beneath my writing

and teaching, if nothing more, has grown in the wake of that big change.[56]

Reynolds Price is writing about savoring, savoring his work and his friends especially. And there are clear signals in the memoir that he savors, too, the person of Christ.

Practical Suggestions

All of us can take some small steps to develop our capacity to simplify, to be attentive and watchful, to savor the experiences of our own unique lives. Consider the following:

Slow down. When we intentionally slow down we open up the possibility for a different quality of time. The *kairos* of which St. Paul speaks is different from the *chronos* which drives most of our calendars and our lives. Instead of dashing for the phone, move deliberately and slowly toward it. Mindfulness during meal times and in the course of usual household chores can also help shape a different awareness of time. Once in a while, try moving through a day in half-time. If you become anxious about the *chronos*, i.e., worried about accomplishing all you've set out for yourself, follow the practice of a Methodist pastor I read about long ago. Each morning at the end of his prayer time he writes a list of all he thinks he ought to do that day. After a prayer for guidance, he crosses out half the list. Over the years this small step has helped him to focus on the few things that really matter.

Remember, small is beautiful. Choose small acts, small bits of your environment to savor, i.e., to really encounter the essence of the thing. When a letter arrives, sit down to read it, visualize the writer, savor the message. I heard of one man who used letters and post cards as book marks. Over the years they served as reminders of the great gift of family and friends that filled his life.

Some years ago, as an adult, I resumed piano lessons. There were many advantages to being an older student, like choosing the composers I wanted to learn. What I was not prepared for was my teacher's direction, from time to time, to concentrate on *one* measure of music, for an entire week. When I objected she asked me if I didn't want to know that measure of music as intimately as I did my best friend. She wanted me to have the experience of savoring the music as the composer had.

Take a midday break. Take some time to step out of the busyness and create a quiet space. Spend a few minutes simply being open to God. Breathe. And then observe your environment. A prayer for midmorning in the official prayer of the Catholic Church includes the following lines:

> Fill us with the radiance of your light;
> may we understand the law you have given us
> and live it with generosity and faith.

Initiate an "examen" at day's end. Establish a practice of reviewing the day (what Ignatius calls the examen) as it is about to end. Identify the moments, events, situations, and people that brought both consolation and desolation. The sorting through can reveal those areas which need redemption in our lives and those areas that are full of grace and cause for gratitude.

Practice gratitude throughout the day. In truth, all is cause for gratitude; *tout est grâce,* St. Thérèse reminds us. A spirit of thanksgiving opens us to all kinds of possibilities, including soul-deep joy, which can be felt physically. *Deo gratias.*

Sixth Essential

LIGHTNESS AND LAUGHTER

Yes, in joy you shall depart,
in peace you shall be brought back;
Mountains and hills shall break out in song before you,
and all the trees of the countryside shall clap their hands.

(ISAIAH 55:12)

MY FAVORITE IMAGE of the Virgin Mary is a statue in the Basilica of the Immaculate Conception in Washington, D.C. As you enter the main portal to the left is a chapel dedicated to Our Lady of Ireland, and in the middle of the chapel is the large white stone statue — many feet high — which dominates the space. Carved from a single slab of stone is a merry looking Mary, enjoying a toddler-size Jesus who sits on her lap, looking as if he could dart off at any moment. Jesus appears to be laughing in the delighted way that small children do. Washington artist Jemilu Mason has captured what I would call a sense of holy mirth.

Laughter is an indicator of lightness of spirit (and ultimately of trust). It signals our enjoyment of God and that we take pleasure in the things of God. Such, however, was not the view of St. Augustine, who condemned laughter (preferring weeping), nor of St. John Chrysostom, who is reputed to have said, "Christ never laughed."[57]

Tears and Laughter: Being Human

In response to those who believe laughter incompatible with a se-rious commitment to the Christian life, German theologian K.-J. Kuschel responds, "Could the one of whom his opponents as-serted that he was a 'glutton and winebibber,' 'a friend of tax collectors and sinners', have made laughter a tabu? That is incon-ceivable. The New Testament knows God's joy, a joy which must necessarily express itself in laughter."[58] And as Thomas Aquinas succinctly pointed out in the *Summa Theologiae,* "Happiness is God's above all."

Spiritual growth is first of all the discovery of what constitutes our humanity, our human consciousness, including our bodili-ness. The expression of deep feelings is certainly one aspect of the fully human person, and humor and laughter are signs of that humanity. In Kuschel's words, "Joy becomes concrete in laughter."

The deep feeling that yields tears does not seem to be a prob-lem. The early church fathers knew that Jesus wept, because several passages of Scripture describe the scenes. Luke 19:41–42 recounts Jesus going up to Jerusalem in great sorrow, accompa-nied by anguished tears. He cries over the holy city, "If this day you only knew what makes for peace." What might that be? Tears certainly have a place, but Thich Nhat Hanh is sure that a smile is an act of peace.[59]

I know a man — Anglo, middle class — who now intentionally smiles and greets African-American men he passes on the street. He does this, he told me (I've taken walks with him), because he has listened to the culture which emanates negativism toward these men. A smile is his small, steady action to show solidarity and to sow some seeds of peace.

The truth is that both tears and laughter put us in touch with our humanity. Yes, Jesus did weep. He wept over Jerusalem, and he wept when his friend Lazarus died. He was "perturbed and deeply troubled," we are told, and he wept (John 11:35).

Were there other occasions? Probably, I think Jesus also wept when the unnamed woman washed his feet with her tears, his tears mingling with hers (Luke 7:37–38). I don't know this to be true, but I imagine it happened that way, a man so alive, so acutely aware of being human. It is entirely possible he wept over Thomas, one of his close followers, who seemed unable or unwilling to fathom the story Jesus was unfolding before him. And what about all the times of sheer exhaustion when he had to get away alone, to get back in touch with the source of his being? Wouldn't tears be a release?

But did he laugh? Were Augustine and the early fathers right?

I return to his humanity. He must have laughed. Humans laugh, period. And the humans depicted in the Bible laugh, although not always for reasons of holy mirth. Take Sarah and Abraham, who laughed most heartily at the discrepancy between God's promise of their impending parenthood and their obvious old age. They laughed out of their sense of reality and out of the possibility that *maybe* reality as they perceived it could be altered. Prof. Kuschel says of this couple that they are not punished, but rather God proceeds with his plan and *laughs with them,* the doubters. If God laughed with Sarah and Abraham, perhaps Jesus laughed with or over the other doubter, Thomas. Such laughter is fundamentally kind and sympathetic.

And he must have laughed over all the funny stuff going on during the course of his ministry. Zacchaeus perched in a sycamore tree, for instance, who made enough of an impression to get mentioned in the rather sparse New Testament narrative (Luke 19:1–10).

Imagine the people on the roof of the house where Jesus was teaching, those inventive friends who removed tiles from the roof and lowered a paralytic, in need of healing, into the presence of Jesus. There must have been shouts of encouragement, clapping, peals of laughter as the daring effort was completed. And the rafters must have resounded with laughter when, at Jesus' urging, the paralytic finally "got up...picked up his stretcher and walked out in front of everyone." We read that the astonished crowd praised God (Mark 2:12). Praising God in biblical literature is not a quiet event. Praise includes song, dance, and musical instruments. Can laughter be far behind such merriment?

Weddings are usually fun. We know of at least one wedding which Jesus attended, where he provided the wedding guests with a flow of vintage wine. How gloriously merry the occasion must have been. How holy. I expect there must have been other wedding celebrations during the course of his peregrinations. And lots of laughter.

Blessed Mirthfulness

"A sense of humor is...a precondition of holiness," writes Doris Donnelly.[60] Holiness is what the spiritual journey is all about — the movement toward God, the Holy One. As we shed the layers of egoism, our true selves are uncovered, and we are readied, step by step, for the encounter of our lives. The first Letter to the Corinthians describes the progress this way. "At present we see indistinctly, as in a mirror, but then face to face. At present I know partially; then I shall know fully as I am fully known" (1 Cor. 13:12). Donnelly says that the God we shall see face to face is very likely to be laughing.[61]

With every passing year I am more convinced that God dearly wants us to be happy — all of us — and to enjoy being with him. Aquinas speaks of all happiness being gathered into God's happiness. That is a powerful image which leads me to think that God enjoys us enjoying him, and to recognize in my own life the God-given prods that urge me to lighten up.

I have learned something about the benefits of lightening one's spirit from the African-American community with whom I worship. We are blessed in our small, white clapboard church with the legacy of spirituals, of clapping, of making a joyful noise. Amazingly, spiritual joy has never been lost in all the years of African-Americans' oppression, of their being on the margins, of doing without. During the worst times of despair, they never lost the gift of laughter. Today, that gift is spilling out to others, to soothe troubled spirits, a sign of abundant beatitude.

Several years ago I noticed a colleague at the bishops' national headquarters had undergone a significant change. A layman noted for his executive drive, he usually had lunch at his desk, worked long hours, expected the same from his staff. Then he began to come regularly to the noon Mass in our small chapel. Not only that, he sang every hymn with enthusiasm and gusto. Overall, he seemed a lot more relaxed. One day I asked him about the change.

He told me he had been attending an African-American church, one noted for its superb gospel choir. One Sunday he "got happy," meaning he was deeply touched with the joy of the Holy Spirit. He knew the exact moment: it happened during a hymn. A woman in the choir hit a high note, ready to sustain it forever (for all eternity, it seemed). It entered somewhere in his soul, he said. And now he's happy, so happy that he's quit his job, has bought a farm, and is more concerned about his *being* than about *achieving*. I expect he's making joyful noises unto the Lord.

God and Play

The concept of play, a close kin of laughter, appears in Hebrew and Christian Scriptures, in the writings of the patristic period, and in the works of the mystics and saints as a form of participation in the life of God. As mentioned earlier we have Jesus' urging that we become like little children. The world of children is largely a world of play which absorbs their attention. It is an imaginative world because they are not overly attached to results. They are open, and so all things are possible.

St. Thérèse of Lisieux, recently named a doctor of the church (only the third woman in Christian history to be so honored), is known for her spiritual theology of "the little way." This means that the small, hardly noticeable tasks of ordinary living, performed with love, become the means of our achieving union with God. Her "little way" is modeled after a child at play. She casts spirituality as a relationship with God in which we are very small children who do not need to achieve very much, but who simply recognize their dependence on God. To practice St. Thérèse's "little way" is a good means of lightening up.[62]

Hugo Rahner, S.J., would agree. In fact he is quite clear that the human person should imitate God at play (meaning God's own creative power) by a lightness of touch, by regard for beauty, by wisdom, and by the sober seriousness of the endeavor. Rahner's playful person, then, is a "grave-merry one." He illustrates this with a delightful mosaic of saints at play. My favorite is the blessed St. Perpetua (martyred by the lions), who in heaven says, "Thanks be to God! As I was merry in the flesh, now here I am merrier still."[63] It is, I think, a question of balance. The state of the world deserves a certain gravitas, but it also needs a sense of humor.

Laughter's Limits

Not all laughter, however, bursts forth from childlike dependence on God. It needs to be situated within a larger framework of ethics and justice. Laughter from a superior stance, directed at those who are vulnerable and weak, is not the kind of laughter that arises from spiritual joy. Strangely, even some of the psalms picture a God who is mocking his enemies with laughter (as in

Psalm 2), hardly the kind of behavior we might want to emulate. What is wanting in such depictions is the quality of mercy. For Christians, according to Professor Kuschel, laughter and ethical self-restraint belong indissolubly together, an echo perhaps of Rahner's grave-merry person. For those who feel particularly committed to the despised and outcast, says Kuschel, there are limits to laughter. His example of inappropriate wrongful laughter is the Nazis who found that jokes and laughter made it easier for them to go to war and to murder Jews in the concentration camps.[64] By contrast, in response to the question that haunts Jews and Christians alike when pondering the Holocaust — namely, *where was God?* — Menachem Rosensaft, a child of Holocaust survivors, said that God was within every Jew who told a story or a joke or sang a melody in a death camp barrack to alleviate a friend's agony. He said the incredible element in the horror of the Holocaust is not the behavior of the murderers, because that is pure evil; it is the behavior of the victims, people who shared their rations and offered comfort. God was with them.[65] And God was probably laughing at the jokes.

God was also with those outside the camps, all the non-Jewish righteous men and women who helped save a fellow human being, as did the villagers of Le Chambon. How could they have sustained the tension of their common mission without a sense of humor? Laughter has the capacity to unite, even when there are differences. It is, in fact, supportive of community.

Spiritual literature through the ages notes that the gift of tears is a sign of the Spirit's presence at a particular time. Sts. Ignatius and Teresa of Avila make special mention of the tears that come with prayerful meditation, a sign perhaps of hearts of stone becoming hearts of flesh. But another gift, a companion to tears, is the gift of laughter. One easily imagines laughter flowing from the fruits of the Spirit (Gal. 5:22–23). The last of the fruitful list — self-control — can create the proper limits.

Practical Suggestions

The practices suggested in the chapter on savoring can help us to lighten our spirits. Consult them and include some of the following:

Linger over the prayer of gratitude. Concentrate on the people closest to you, holding up their positive qualities. This has the effect of shifting emphasis from judgment to appreciation, a shift that lightens the spirit.

Practice smiling. If you take a solitude walk, you are still likely to encounter people along the way. Greet them with a smile and let the smile linger with you. This applies to other kinds of walking, along busy city streets, for example. Look at people you pass by and smile. Soon you will notice them greeting you and smiling. Remember, these are small peace-making acts.

Be with people who laugh. Connect with people who have the gift of laughter. Invite them to join with your own life events; respond to their invitations. Remember, laughing together is a community-building activity.

Ponder the Scriptures. Doris Donnelly suggests that we look for humor in the Scriptures — which is there, of course. "Relax," she writes. "Read the Bible open to the possibility that something new is happening — that God lives in laughter, lightness, freedom, spontaneity, and some unfamiliar places."[66]

Seventh Essential

SURRENDER

"My grace is sufficient for you, for power is made perfect in weakness." (2 CORINTHIANS 12:9)

The Little Way of Surrender

IN MOST AREAS OF OUR LIFE maturity is measured by our individual initiative, self-reliance, self-direction, and sometimes personal achievement. St. Thérèse of Lisieux alerts us to the difference in regard to our spiritual life. Her "little way," mentioned in the previous chapter, has had a profound influence on spiritual seekers in the twentieth century. For Thérèse it is surrender, not achievement, that is the essence of the spiritual life.

At first, postmodern men and women might find her message difficult to comprehend. But for those who find inspiration in the Scriptures, Thérèse's metaphor of our relationship with God as that of small children dependent on the love and care of a parent rings true. She writes that when she found the words "Whosoever is a little one, let him come to me," she felt the confidence to draw near to God. Continuing her scriptural search she found more, "You shall be carried at the breast and upon the knees: as one whom the mother caresses, so will I comfort you." This profound awareness of dependence formed her theological and spiritual foundation.[67]

Twelve Steps

Thérèse's way of simplicity and surrender is one well known to members of Alcoholics Anonymous — AA. This spiritually based fellowship began in 1935 in Akron, Ohio, where two men with severe alcoholism — one a surgeon and one a New York broker — met. They are considered cofounders of the AA fellowship.

The basic principles, known as the Twelve Steps, are derived from the fields of religion and medicine.[68] The first step, "We admitted we were powerless over alcohol — that our lives had become unmanageable," and the second, "We came to believe that a Power greater than ourselves could restore us to sanity," illustrate the crucial relationship between powerlessness and a Higher Power. It is the meaning of the passage from the second Letter to the Corinthians which introduces this chapter, and it is also the heart of Thérèse's little way of surrender to God.

Acknowledging one's total dependence on a Higher Power — surrendering — does not come easily. The AA literature recounts how the less than desperate alcoholics who tried AA in the early days, i.e., those who were still functioning, did not succeed precisely because they could not make the admission of hopelessness and helplessness. Many inner obstacles hindered their sincerely acknowledging a Higher Power, among them indifference, prejudice, and defiance. In particular defiance seemed impenetrable. The AA founders recalled that in the past they had not asked what God's will for them was; instead they had been telling God what it might be.[69] Their challenge was to transform defiance into reliance, and humility was found to be the transforming agent. "True humility and an open mind can lead us to faith, and every AA meeting is an assurance that God will restore us to sanity if we rightly relate ourselves to Him."[70] True humility means we are able to deal with our own limitations and the limitations of others, recognizing that God is in life and that we are not in charge. Humility brings serenity and hope, inner peace and real energy.[71]

Humility and surrender are not, however, marks of a passive life. On the contrary. AA emphasizes that *action* is necessary to cut away the self-will which always blocks the entry of God into one's life. Certainly in Christianity — and in other religions as well — faith without action is not at all sufficient. In AA the meeting, a form of authentic community, provides the vehicle for activating faith. Thérèse discovered the same truth:

> I have labored above all to love God, but it was in loving
> him that I discovered the hidden meaning of these words:
> "Not everyone who says Lord, Lord, shall enter the king-
> dom of heaven, but he that does the will of my Father"...I
> understood now that true charity consists in bearing all my
> neighbor's defects, in not being surprised by their mistakes,
> but by being edified by their smallest virtues. Above all I've
> learned that charity must not be kept shut up in the heart,
> for "no one lights a candle and puts it in a hidden place,
> or under a bushel...." The candle, it seems to me, rep-
> resents the charity that enlightens and gladdens, not only
> those who are dearest to us, but likewise all of our brothers
> and sisters everywhere.[72]

The AA prayer captures her meaning: "God grant me the serenity to accept the things I cannot change, courage to change the things I can, and wisdom to know the difference. Thy will be done." It is essentially an action prayer.

Thy will be done. A friend once said to me that this is the most problematic line in the Lord's Prayer. Even though Christians re-peat the line frequently — daily or more — he doubted if many people really mean what they pray. He said that he knew that for him the words really meant, "Help me, God, to achieve my will." I understood him completely.

How often do we go to God in prayer with a question or a problem, already convinced we know the answer (although we may courteously refrain from saying so aloud)? Are we really seeking confirmation of what we've already decided? And maybe seeking a little action on God's part? When we do this we are closed to the newness of the Spirit's leadings.

But authentic prayer and surrender is anything but closed and static. It is full of dynamism, as we see in the story of Jesus in the garden just hours before his death. The story begins with the Passover meal which Jesus shared with his closest friends. After the meal they make their way across the Kidron valley to a garden on the Mount of Olives. Jesus is clearly troubled. He needs prayer, but he also needs companionship. His friends, tired perhaps from food and wine and the long walk, find a spot to rest. Their rest quickly becomes a deep sleep. Jesus moves away from them and prays a prayer of anguish. He can see his life crescendoing toward an explosive conclusion. His first prayer beseeches the Holy One, his Father, to change the course of what seems inevitable: "Take this cup away from me," adding, "Not what I will, but what you will." He is not indifferent to all that lies ahead. "My soul is sorrowful unto death," he cries. He prays for a while, then goes to his friends who are still sleeping. No help there. He returns again to beseeching God. He prays for a while, then goes to his friends who remain unaware of all that he is going through. During those moments or hours in the garden Jesus seems to undergo a profound change. He begins his prayer wanting to be spared from the horrors that await him; but before the officials come to arrest him he surrenders to the God of Abraham, Isaac, and Jacob, to the God of his ancestor David. He goes to meet his executioners (Mark 14:32–42). There is an important lesson here: true surrender does not happen all at once.

A Story of Surrender: Joseph Cardinal Bernardin

Those of us who knew Joseph Bernardin, the cardinal archbishop of Chicago, and those who watched from afar, were deeply affected by the example of his last years on earth. Beginning in 1993 he faced challenge after challenge to the life he had known for so many years. The first of these was the false accusation that Bernardin had sexually abused Steven Cook in Cincinnati, Ohio, when Bernardin was the bishop there — years before — and Cook was a seminarian. The charge came without warning. At the time the cardinal was chairman of the Marriage and Family Life Committee, for which I was responsible as director of the office which staffed that committee. The charge, and the publicity, came a few days before the November meeting of the American bishops, where the cardinal was to present a document we had prepared about marriage and family life.[73]

Despite the storm all around him he insisted on meeting what he saw as his responsibility. Humbly he stood before his brother bishops and won a unanimous vote of approval for the document. He appeared to carry all these burdens lightly, but later he wrote that he was "devastated" by the accusation. Weighed down by the injustice of it all, he approached the situation the way he had approached everything in recent years, by turning to prayer. Recently, he said, he had been praying to learn to let go — to really let go — and empty himself. Could this horror be a step in that emptying, he wondered? Within the far recesses of his soul he heard the Lord's words, "The truth will set you free" (John 8:32).

That awareness set his course, not only in regard to the false allegations, but also in regard to the cancer that would erupt in a few years. The meaning of his life became ever more clear: he was a man committed to the truth. He surrendered to the truth and to everything which that surrender brought in its wake. "My faith reassured me that the truth was all I had, and all that I really needed. It would be my rod and my staff through the dark valley in the months ahead."[74] He took that rod and staff to press conferences where he answered questions directly and without any "spin" whatsoever. He took them to the meetings of

the National Conference of Catholic Bishops, where he continued to meet every responsibility in spite of the weight of sorrow.
He took them to his meeting with Steven Cook after the abuse
charges had been dropped. (He also took with him a heart full of
forgiveness and compassion for his accuser.)

The meeting took place at the cardinal's initiative. Cook, who
was gravely ill with AIDS, apologized for the false accusation.
Bernardin said Mass for the dying young man and anointed him
with the sacrament of the sick. The cardinal later described
this experience of reconciliation and peace as "an afternoon of
grace."[75]

Some months after the reconciliation Cardinal Bernardin was
diagnosed with pancreatic cancer. This new challenge centered
him even more deeply in the way of truth as he faced the
ultimate mystery of life and death:

> In the final analysis our participation in the paschal mys-
> tery — in the suffering, death, and resurrection of Jesus —
> brings a certain freedom: the freedom to let go, to surrender
> ourselves to the living God, to place ourselves completely in
> his hands.... The more we cling to ourselves and to others,
> the more we try to control our destiny — the more we lose
> the true sense of our lives, the more we are impacted by the
> futility of it all. It's precisely in letting go, in entering into
> complete union with the Lord, in letting him take over, that
> we discover our true selves.[76]

Bernardin is clear that surrender affects not only "my person"
but also the environments we inhabit. "Our years of living as
Christians will be years of suffering for and with other people.
Like Jesus we will love others only if we walk in the valley of
darkness — the dark valley of sickness, the dark valley of moral
dilemmas, the dark valley of oppressive structures and diminished
rights."[77]

As the cancer moved through his body and the treatment ceased, the people of Chicago, and indeed the world, pinned bits of green ribbon to their clothes — green being the color of hope — and prayed with him and with one another the Prayer of St. Francis.

> Lord, make me an instrument of your peace.
> Where there is hatred, let me sow love.
> Where there is injury, pardon.
> Where there is doubt, faith.
> Where there is despair, hope.
> Where there is darkness, light.
> Where there is sadness, joy.
> O Divine Master,
> grant that I may not so much seek
> to be consoled, as to console;
> to be understood, as to understand;
> to be loved, as to love;
> for it is in giving that we receive,
> it is in pardoning that we are pardoned.
> It is in dying that we are born to eternal life.

This prayer of total surrender and vibrant truth about the nature of spiritual reality is a cherished prayer of the AA fellowship. Its reminder that in dying we are born to life is a precious truth of the world's great religions.

New Life and Surrender

Every woman who has labored to bring forth a baby knows that a moment comes when she faces the inevitability of birth and surrenders herself to it. The truth rises in us: there is no turning back. A dynamic process is underway and life is ready to burst forth. Only a direct intervention can change or thwart the forward thrust of the life force. The process is painful to some de-gree, even with the relaxation practices and breathing techniques that many employ to ease the way into new life. Surrender can be eased but is rarely without some form of pain. (Remember Jesus in the garden.)

One of the most important contributions for grappling with the relationship between birth and death and with the spiritual truth of surrender which underlies both events is *The Tibetan Book of Living and Dying.* It is a book of genuine hope, helpful to those preparing for the birth of a child and helpful to those preparing for the continuing birth of the spiritual life. The deep and too often unrecognized truth that letting go is the path to real freedom and that in learning to live in real freedom is the truest preparation for our own death is the central core of the book. We learn that the great masters of Buddhist teaching (who inhabit the book) would not have discovered their inner strength had they not faced great difficulties and obstacles.

It is essential, the author insists, to reflect on impermanence and change. We are part of that change, for we all are dying, moment by moment. For some it will happen sooner rather than later. There is an echo of Teresa of Avila here who reminds us that all things pass away.

Not only is everything impermanent, but everything is also interdependent. "True spirituality...is to be aware that if we are interdependent with everything and everyone else, even our smallest, least significant thought, word and actions have real consequences throughout the universe."[78]

Our ordinary actions matter. What we think matters. Each Sunday Catholics around the world, in the context of the Eu-charist, pray the ancient Confiteor — our prayer of confession. In it we confess not only to the God of the universe and of galaxies yet to be discovered, but to all who gather with us in the act of Sunday worship. We confess to those close at hand with whom we share life and worship about the ways we have wronged them. The psychological soundness of the prayer is evident in the small succinct phrase, "through my fault." All these offenses which we confess are our own faults. We do not confess our unhappy childhood or our unfortunate personality traits, but rather we take responsibility for our selves, without blaming others.

The psychological soundness is also evident in the phrase, "I have sinned in thought, word, and deed." Some moralists have tended to interpret the "thought" part in terms of sexuality, but it is much more than that. How we think of one another, and ourselves, matters a great deal. If we are reducing one another, in our minds, to people of small matter, of little consequence, then it is possible to deny the equality of the races or the sexes or various states of life. If I think about others in stereotypes, I can more easily dismiss them, justify my anger toward them, and rationalize my tearing them down. The Confiteor does not let us off the hook. It tells us that the sins occur in two ways: what we do (and think) and what we fail to do. When we turn away from injustice and the pain of others we allow evil to thrive. The Holocaust Museum in Washington, D.C., reminds us that evil happens when good people look the other way.[79] It is essential that we face the reality all around us. It is essential that we be responsible. Being responsible can lead to resurrection.

The Hindu Holy Scriptures, the Upanishads, tell us that it is possible to have a personal, utterly nonconceptual revelation of what we are, why we are here, and how we should act, which amounts in the end to nothing less than a new life, a new birth, almost, you could say, a resurrection. One need not travel to India or Tibet, however, for the realization to occur.

Reynolds Price's story (which appeared in the chapter on savoring) is instructive in this regard. He advises that anyone confronted with a grave illness or other physical or psychic trauma come to terms with a primary fact: namely, you will *never* be the person you were before the trauma, even though all the people who love you will try to convince you that you can be the way you used to be. "Your mate, your children, your friends at work — anyone who knew and loved you in your old life — will be hard at work in the fierce endeavor to revive your old self, the self they recall with love or respect.... Their care is often a brake on the way you must go. Yet, if you don't discover that next appropriate incarnation of who you must be, and then *become* that person at a stiff trot, you'll be no good whatever." About himself he says, "The kindest thing anyone could have done for me, once I'd finished five weeks' radiation, would have been to look me square in the eye and say this clearly, "Reynolds Price is dead. Who will you be now? Who can you be and how can you get there, double time?"[80]

Please note. To get to the point of transformation, and the surrender it entailed, Price was helped and held by prayer, and by a single vision of Christ that offered healing. The vision came unbidden. He did not doubt it. He has never forgotten it. There was also an auditory experience of the Divine. In the midst of great physical and psychic pain Price cried out to the Being he presumed was God, "What now?" He heard a single word response, "More." He realized that he was being given the choice of Deuteronomy: "I have set before you life and death, the blessing and the curse. Choose life, then, that you and your descendants may live" (Deut. 30:19). Ultimately surrender is not about giving up, but about choosing life. Suffering, in some form, is often the context for surrender, because it can move us to be really open. Where we are extremely vulnerable we encounter our greatest strength. Our hearts of stone are transformed to flesh.

SUFFERING

All that day long I spent the hours with suffering.
I woke to find her sitting by my bed.

She stalked my footsteps while time slowed to timeless,
tortured my sight, came close in what was said.

She asked no more than that, beneath unwelcome,
I might be mindful of her grant of grace.
I still can smile, amused, when I remember
how I surprised her when I kissed her face.[81]

The embrace of suffering in the poem is the surrender that signals
new life.

Loss involves not only our own individual suffering, but the
suffering of others. Loss is all around us. We watch the diminish-
ment of our loved ones from diseases of all kinds, physical and
mental. One of the cruelest is Alzheimer's disease because the
essence of the person we've known, with whom we've shared life's
intimacies, hopes, and plans, is gone. Only a shell remains. The
right order of things is skewed.

Ellen, a teacher, painter, and poet, an only child whose father died decades ago, enjoyed a close and lively relationship
with her mother, who was intelligent and independent and vitally
interested in the world around her. Then, at age eighty, everything changed. She sold her home and moved to a retirement
community near her daughter. Almost immediately, the symp-
toms of Alzheimer's appeared, although Ellen now says that they
were evident earlier, but overlooked, since her mother functioned
fairly well in her familiar space. But a strange building provided
no props; her disorientation increased until she required a nurs-
ing home. She was terrified at what was happening to her; she
asked for answers, and there were none. She thought Ellen was a
waitress who looked like her daughter.

Ellen tried to write her way out of the growing grief, which
was only intensified by her mother's death. It took a year of
her mother being totally gone before Ellen could surrender her
to God.

ANNIVERSARY

What ceremony, then, to mark this day?
What rite, what words, what gestures
to celebrate and mourn
this first year's passage?

I sat at the piano
and played her music
with fingers strangely calm
and hands finding the right places
on the keyboard.
I sent her her afternoons
of Beethoven's minuet
and Mozart's sonata,
sent the notes clear out the screen door
and up to a sky gray and blue
with undecided clouds.
And as I filled the hour
with notes and chords,
arpeggios and trills,
I gave the gift of shared music
to both of us.

When the day opened
into early afternoon,
I knew the moment of her quiet flight
a year ago had come again,
and I gave her over to God
forever this time.
This time
I let her go
to His peace
where she can smile forever
and where I hope

when the wind is right
she can hear the remembered melodies
of Mozart
from my piano.[82]

Practical Suggestions

Surrender negativity. Surrender to God (or the Higher Power) all the grasping, clinging, and ignorance that entraps all of us at some time. The serenity prayer of AA can help us to become conscious of these blocks to surrender.

Sincerely pray to know God's will. Ask for the strength to align your life with that will. The practice of Ignatian discernment discussed in the first chapter can be of assistance.

Pray for others. Spend time praying for the peace and welfare of others; we are helped to realize our interdependence in so doing.

Practice willingness. This movement of the Spirit is the opposite of willfulness. It involves small acts of surrender by choosing another's preference over one's own. It might mean keeping quiet rather than giving a "bright retort." It might mean doing something a loved one prefers. The key to this practice is awareness, not passivity. It is, in truth, a "little way."

Memento mori. This translates, "Remember you will die," and it is the name of a remarkable little novel by Muriel Spark. Remembering this truth about our human existence can have a very beneficial effect and can enhance the quality of our everyday life. We can take steps to remember: practice the breathing meditation, perhaps with the mantra suggested by the

Dominican friar (Detach; let go); reflect on Joseph Bernardin's insight that death is a friend.

💪 *Savor the details of ordinary life.* Review the fifth chapter, on savoring. This is a component of surrender. And remember, surrender is not passivity, but a doorway to gentle realism.

AFTERWORD

B Y NOW YOU ARE AWARE that the seven essentials presented here are not distinct from one another. They are closely related. Mentors and guides will point us to times of solitude and silence. They will also encourage us to be part of an authentic community, for it is in such communal settings that the insights of our solitude are tested. Savoring and laughter can help us discover the sacred which is all around us: in nature, in people, in works of art, and in the ordinary litter of our daily environments. Clyde Connell's discovery of beauty in the soil of Louisiana with its red clay and broken sticks is a reminder that we often fail to see into the heart of things, and all the possibilities therein.

Gratitude is foundational. It is our compass on the journey to God and is woven into all seven essentials. It releases genuine humility which is key in our surrender to the One who created us and sustains us and who awaits us when the journey is over.

Journeys are full of adventure and discovery, full of wonder. But there comes the time when we are ready for home. The essentials which have been lighting the way for us will guide us over the threshold to that place we have always known in the depths of our souls.

THE HOMECOMING

The spirit, newly freed from earth,
is all amazed at the surprise
of her belonging: suddenly
as native to eternity
to see herself, to realize

the heritage that lets her be
at home where all this glory lies.

By naught foretold could she have guessed
such welcome home: the robe, the ring,
music and endless banqueting,
these people hers; this place of rest
known, as of long remembering
herself a child of God and pressed
with warm endearments to His breast.[83]

Notes

1. Thomas Kelly, *A Testament of Devotion* (New York: Harper & Row, 1941), 21.

2. Ibid., 18–19.

3. Steere as cited in ibid., 19.

4. Dr. Dana Greene has authored and edited a number of books about Evelyn Underhill. See *Artist of the Infinite Life* (New York: Crossroad, 1990); *Evelyn Underhill: Modern Guide to the Ancient Quest for the Holy* (New York: State University of New York Press, 1988); *Fragments from an Inner Life* (Harrisburg, Pa.: Morehouse, 1993).

5. Evelyn Underhill, *Practical Mysticism* (New York: E. P. Dutton), 3.

6. Ibid., 31.

7. Langston Hughes, "The Negro Speaks of Rivers," in *Treasury of American Poetry*, ed. Nancy Sullivan (Garden City, N.Y.: Doubleday, 1978), 500.

8. Jessica Powers, "To Live with the Spirit," in *Selected Poetry of Jessica Powers*, ed. Regina Siegfried and Robert Morneau (Kansas City, Mo.: Sheed & Ward, 1989), 38. Now available from ICS Publications, 2131 Lincoln Rd. NE, Washington, DC 20002.

9. Dolores R. Leckey, "Women of the Church: Today's Spiritual Leaders," in *Sisters Today* 68, no. 2 (March 1996): 85.

10. Kenneth Leech, "Is Spiritual Direction Losing Its Bearings?" in *The Tablet*, May 22, 1993. Cited by John Crossin, O.S.F.S., in *Friendship: The Key to Spiritual Growth* (Mahwah, N.J.: Paulist, 1997), 70.

11. Ibid., 71.

12. Aelred of Rievaulx, *Spiritual Friendship* (Kalamazoo, Mich.: Cistercian Publications, 1977), 93.

13. A brief biographical note can be found in *Ignatius Loyola: Spiritual Exercises*, ed. Joseph H. Tetlow, S.J. (New York: Crossroad, 1982).

14. Ibid., 22.

15. Ibid., 38.

16. Eugenia Ginzburg, *Within the Whirlwind*, trans. Ian Boland (New York: Harcourt Brace Jovanovich, 1981), 115.

17. Ibid., 420.

18. Dolores Leckey, *The Ordinary Way* (New York: Crossroad, 1982), 77.

19. May Sarton, *Journal of a Solitude* (New York: W. W. Norton, 1973), 11.

20. "Counsel for Silence," in *Selected Poetry of Jessica Powers*, 85.

21. See Leckey, *The Ordinary Way*, 79.

22. Thich Nhat Hanh, *Living Buddha, Living Christ* (New York: G. P. Putnam's Sons, 1995), 153.

23. See John Main, O.S.B., *Word into Silence* (Mahwah, N.J.: Paulist, 1981).

24. Contemplative Outreach, Ltd. (P.O. Box 737, 9 William St., Butler, NJ 07405), is a network of faith communities, Catholic in origin, ecumenical in scope, committed to renewing the contemplative dimension of the Gospel in everyday life.

25. Main, *Word into Silence*, 9.

26. Richard of St. Victor, *Selected Writings on Contemplation*, ed. C. Kirchberger (Faber & Faber, 1957), 102; cited by John Main in *Word into Silence*, 20.

27. Karl Rahner, *Encounter with Silence* (Westminster, Md.: Newman, 1966), 46.

28. Ibid., 48.

29. Ibid., 57.

30. Max Picard, *The World of Silence* (Chicago: Henry Regnery, 1952), 25.

31. Jean Sulivan, "The Beginning of Silence," in *Cross Currents* 24, no. 4 (Winter 1985–86): 436.

32. Dolores Leckey, *Winter Music: A Life of Jessica Powers* (Kansas City, Mo.: Sheed & Ward, 1992), 6–7.

33. "The House at Rest," in *Selected Poetry of Jessica Powers*, 122.

34. This account first appeared in *Church*, Fall 1998, a publication of the National Pastoral Life Center, under the title "Resting in God: A Different Kind of Jubilee Celebration."

35. Edward Fischer, *Life in the Afternoon* (Mahwah, N.J.: Paulist, 1987), 82.

36. John O'Donohue, *Anam Cara* (New York: HarperCollins, 1997), 85.

37. Margaret Kabalin Leckey, from an unpublished essay, "On Gardening."

38. O'Donohue, *Anam Cara*, 192.

39. Ibid., 119.

40. A Sangha is an intentional community of people, in the Buddhist tradition, where common spiritual and religious practices form the routines of daily living. As in a monastery or a church, the Sangha provides communal support for the spiritual/religious journey.

41. Thich Nhat Hanh, *Living Buddha, Living Christ*, 61.

42. Main, *Word into Silence*, 78.

43. Annette Kane, Executive Director of the National Council of Catholic Women, and with her husband, a long time member of The Teams of Our Lady, provided this account.

44. Thich Nhat Hanh, *Living Buddha, Living Christ*, 65.

45. Main, *Word into Silence*, 78.

46. Loren Eiseley, *The Immense Journey* (New York: Vintage Books, 1946), 197.

47. Mary Oliver, *American Primitive* (Boston: Back Bay, 1978), 10–11.

48. Pablo Neruda, *Odes to Common Things,* trans. Ken Krabbenhoft (Boston: Little, Brown, 1994), 103.

49. These testimonies were written to me in a response to a column I wrote in 1987 (for Catholic News Service) asking readers to write to me about their experience of God in everyday life.

50. Information about Clyde Connell was found in an obituary written by Roberta Smith, which appeared in the *New York Times,* May 10, 1998.

51. "Detachment and Non-Attachment in Dogen and Eckhart," an unpublished paper by James D. Campbell, O.P.

52. *Selected Poetry of Jessica Powers,* 104.

53. Catherine Walsh, "Perspectives," in *America,* January 31, 1998, 5.

54. Vita Sackville-West, *All Passion Spent* (London: Virago, 1931), 141.

55. This explication of the child at play is from Leckey, *The Ordinary Way,* chapter 6.

56. Reynolds Price, *A Whole New Life: An Illness and a Healing* (New York: Atheneum, 1994), 189–190.

57. Quoted by David R. Blumenthal in a review of K.-J. Kuschel's *Laughter: A Theological Reflection,* trans. J. Bowden (New York: Continuum, 1994), in *Cross Currents* (Summer 1995).

58. Ibid.

59. All of Thich Nhat Hanh's books refer to smiling as a pathway to peace. See *Living Buddha, Living Christ* for a helpful listing of books.

60. See chapter 6, "Laughing," in Doris Donnelly, *Spiritual Fitness* (San Francisco: HarperSanFrancisco, 1993).

61. Donnelly refers her readers to Psalm 2, which describes God as laughing.

62. See *The Story of a Soul: The Autobiography of St. Thérèse of Lisieux.* Available from ICS Publications, Washington, D.C.

63. See Hugo Rahner, *Man at Play* (New York: Herder and Herder, 1967). Also Leckey, *The Ordinary Way,* chapter 6, "Play."

64. Review of *Laughter: A Theological Reflection* in *Cross Currents,* 124.

65. Rosensaft's remarks were made at a ceremony at the Holocaust Museum in Washington, D.C.

66. Dr. Donnelly has a number of suggestions for "exercising laughter" in her book *Spiritual Fitness.*

67. John Kirvan, *Simply Surrender* (Notre Dame, Ind.: Ave Maria, 1996), 46.

68. Information about AA, its history and tenets, is found in *Twelve Steps and Twelve Traditions* (Alcoholics Anonymous World Services, Inc.)

69. Ibid., 31.

70. Ibid., 33.

71. Joan Chittister, O.S.B., recounted by Robert F. Morneau in *Humility* (Winona, Minn.: St. Mary's Press, 1997), 28.

72. Kirvan, *Simply Surrender,* 201–3.

73. The document, *Follow the Way of Love,* is available from the USCC Office of Publishing Services, Washington, D.C.

74. Joseph Cardinal Bernardin, *The Gift of Peace* (Chicago: Loyola University Press, 1997), 23.

75. Ibid., 34–41.

76. Ibid., 48.

77. Ibid., 49.

78. Sogyal Rinpoche, *The Tibetan Book of Living and Dying* (San Francisco: HarperSanFrancisco, 1993), 39.

79. Dolores Leckey on "The Confiteor." This reflection appeared in *Selected Texts from the 1996 National Lay Forum* (Washington, D.C.: Secretariat for Family, Laity, Women and Youth–NCCB).

80. Price, *A Whole New Life,* 184.

81. "Suffering," in *Selected Poetry of Jessica Powers,* 106.

82. "Anniversary," an unpublished poem by Ellen R. Collins. Used with permission.

83. "The Homecoming," in *Selected Poetry of Jessica Powers,* 53.

OF RELATED INTEREST

Joyce Rupp
DEAR HEART, COME HOME
The Path of Midlife Spirituality

Joyce Rupp shares her own midlife journey — with honesty and insight that readers will identify with and benefit from. Filled with stories, poetry, and guided visualizations, this popular author's newest book is a visual feast.

0-8245-1556-0; $13.95

Henri J. M. Nouwen
LIFE OF THE BELOVED
Henri Nouwen sheds light on the challenge of living a spiritual life in a secular world.

0-8245-1184-0; $14.95

Anthony De Mello
WALKING ON WATER
Christian wisdom blends with Eastern insights to help us experience the greatest miracle of all: the peace of God that passes all understanding.

0-8245-1737-7; $12.95

Please support your local bookstore, or call 1-800-395-0690.
For a free catalog, please write us at
THE CROSSROAD PUBLISHING COMPANY
370 LEXINGTON AVENUE, NEW YORK, NY 10017

We hope you enjoyed *Seven Essentials for the Spiritual Journey.*
Please share with us *your* essentials for the Journey.

crossroad